100 THINGS
MICHIGAN FANS
SHOULD KNOW & DO
BEFORE THEY DIE

Angelique Chengelis

TRIUMPH
BOOKS

Library of Congress Cataloging-in-Publication Data

Chengelis, Angelique, 1964–
   100 things Michigan fans should know & do before they die / Angelique Chengelis.
      p. cm.
   ISBN 978-1-60078-779-9
   1. University of Michigan—Football—History. 2. Michigan Wolverines (Football team)—History. 3. Michigan Wolverines (Football team)—Miscellanea. I. Title. II. Title: One hundred things Michigan fans should know and do before they die.
   GV958.U52863C44 2012
   796.332'630977435—dc23
                                        2012025831

This book is available in quantity at special discounts for your group or organization. For further information, contact:
   Triumph Books LLC
   814 North Franklin Street
   Chicago, Illinois 60610
   (312) 337-0747
   www.triumphbooks.com

Printed in U.S.A.
ISBN: 978-1-60078-779-9
Design by Patricia Frey
Photos courtesy of AP Images unless otherwise indicated

To Michigan fans everywhere

Contents

Foreword

Today she is my friend, but before she was my friend, Angelique Chengelis earned my respect as a sportswriter who practiced her craft in a way that honored her profession. As dedicated as the best of her peers, she is very insightful, very knowledgeable, and very passionate about many sports, but none more so than Michigan football.

Now she has written a book for Michigan fans that scans the entire history of what is arguably the greatest tradition in college football.

It began with a game against Racine on May 30, 1879, and now, 130 years later, it is a program that has won more games and possesses a higher winning percentage than any other school.

The showcase for this great tradition is the crown jewel, Michigan Stadium. The colors are maize and blue. The symbols are the winged helmet, the Block M, and the M Ring. The incomparable sound is "The Victors," the greatest fight song ever written. Angelique writes about these traditions as well as national championships and Rose Bowl games. She has selected what she considers our greatest games, and she writes about many of our great players and of the men who coached and administered football here. You will especially enjoy her stories about our Heisman Trophy winners—Tom Harmon, Desmond Howard, and Charles Woodson, as well as President Gerald Ford.

She also revisits some of the most controversial moments in our history—moments that remain so unforgettable and, for some, so painful.

There is enough trivia for the most devoted fan, and if you want to experience game day in Ann Arbor, go on the road for Big Ten football, or march in the Michigan band, it is all here. The great rivalries and the incredible come-from-behind victories are here as well; and, yes, there are even some of those other days, those "days from hell" when our hearts were broken—only because time ran out on the men of Michigan.

She has covered it all or at least a big part of it, and she has reminded those who read her book why that great old stadium is filled to capacity every Saturday in the fall when some other team comes to Ann Arbor hoping to beat Michigan. They come with love in their heart for the Wolverines, and they come expecting excellence, and they come with an absolute certainty that the guys in maize and blue will win today. But deep down in their heart of hearts, most would admit they come for other reasons, too.

They come because they love this great old school, the University of Michigan; and they love Ann Arbor; and they cherish their memories here; and they want to be here to hear the "Star-Spangled Banner" as that flag is raised at the south end; and they want to be here when those winged helmets begin to emerge from the only tunnel in this place. And they are here knowing that when the Michigan team takes the field and runs under that banner and the band plays *that* song—"The Victors"—there is absolutely no place in this world they would rather be; and they are here because they are part of this tradition; and they are here to help insure that it never dies.... I know it never will.

—Lloyd H. Carr
Ann Arbor, Michigan
March 16, 2009

Acknowledgments

The most enjoyable aspect of working on a project like this book was the interaction with players past and present that such an undertaking absolutely requires. After all, who could offer a better perspective on Michigan football and the things fans should know about the program than those who helped build upon its foundation? So to all of those players who gave me their time, I owe a great deal of thanks.

One of things I never quite realized since my days covering Michigan football for the *Detroit News* began in 1992 is that I have accumulated a lot of Michigan-related "stuff" through the years. My bookshelves are filled with game-day programs and those from bowls, there are media guides from the Big Ten Conference and every other team in the league, there are DVDs of individual Michigan games, and, of course, several devoted to the Michigan–Ohio State game.

But mostly there are a lot of books that proved essential in researching for this book. All were extremely helpful.

Among them, *A Legacy of Champions: The Story of the Men Who Built University of Michigan Football* offered plenty of insights into the minds of three coaches—Fielding H. Yost, Fritz Crisler (I was fortunate enough to research and write that chapter), and Bo Schembechler. Jerry Green's *University of Michigan Football Vault* was—well, how can one say it?—a vault, a treasure of all things Michigan football.

The *Detroit News* published *Amazing Blue: The Michigan Wolverines' Unforgettable 1997 Championship Season*, which refreshed memories of a unique season. Bo Schembechler's *Michigan Memories: Inside Bo Schembechler's Football Scrapbook* brought a favorite voice back to life page by page.

Other sources of information were Bruce Madej's *Michigan Champions of the West*, Jim Brandstatter's *Tales from Michigan Stadium*, John Kyrk's *Natural Enemies*, Joe Falls' *Bo Schembechler: Man in Motion*, and Bill Cromartie's *The Big One*.

The archives of the *Detroit News*, the *Detroit Free Press*, and the Bentley Library were endless sources of assistance for anecdotes and quotes. And who can do research these days without the Internet?

Also, the always helpful Dave Ablauf from Michigan's sports information department was helpful, yet again.

Finally, some thanks on a more personal level. As always, my mother and siblings, Stephanie, Gregory, and Stratin, provided a great deal of support. And I owe a lot of thanks to my husband, David, whose interest in this project and patience were absolutely vital and greatly, greatly—is there room for one more?—greatly appreciated.

1 Bo Schembechler: Legendary Coach

Bo Schembechler arrived on the Michigan campus in 1969 during a time of political and social unrest, particularly in Ann Arbor, where activism was a vital part of the culture.

Schembechler, though, was a football man. He wasn't interested in politics or protests. He was interested in one thing: football. And he was interested in rebuilding a Michigan program that had endured losing seasons in six of the previous 11 years.

So in came Schembechler, who once referred to himself as the "short-haired guy who believed in discipline and hard work." He took over the team in 1969, having been hired by athletics director Don Canham. Schembechler became head coach at Miami (Ohio), his alma mater, in 1963 and won two Mid-American Conference titles.

When he arrived in Ann Arbor, the knock on Michigan was that the Wolverines were not tough. Having a team not considered "tough" was not something Schembechler would or could tolerate.

On the first day of spring practice, he delivered a classic Schembechler speech that caught the attention of all the players. "Now you listen to me, all of you," he said to them. "I do not care if you are white or black or Irish or Italian or Catholic or Jewish or liberal or conservative. From this point on, I will treat you all exactly the same—like dogs!"

During that preseason, Schembechler and his coaches came up with the now well-known, famous slogan, "Those who stay will be champions." The sign was placed above the locker room door. Many left that first season, unable to cope with Schembechler's brutal workouts and practices. One player who left wrote in marker

1

Any self-respecting book on the greatest things about Michigan football must begin with Bo Schembechler. Photo courtesy of Per Kjeldsen.

on that original sign: "And those who quit will be doctors, lawyers, and captains of industry."

Many years later, Schembechler said that of all the teams he had coached, that '69 team had every right to "resent" him. Those players had not come to Michigan to play for Schembechler, after all, and he was exceptionally tough on them.

But all these years later, his players speak lovingly and with tremendous respect for their coach.

"The thing about Bo was, he had a perception of being this real tough guy, and he portrayed that picture to everyone on the outside," said former All-America defensive back Tom Curtis. "But once you got to know Bo, he was just the nicest and the most caring person that you could imagine."

Schembechler's arrival at Michigan ushered in a new era of the Michigan–Ohio State rivalry, as well. Schembechler had played for Woody Hayes at Miami in 1949 and then became a graduate assistant under Hayes at Ohio State in 1951 and later an assistant coach from 1958 to 1962.

This coaching rivalry between teacher and student began in 1969, stretched a decade, and became known as the "10-Year War." Michigan went 5–4–1 against Ohio State during the "war" between Woody and Bo, and it all started with an incredible opening matchup in Ann Arbor. Ohio State, ranked No. 1 and riding a 22-game winning streak, was a 17-point favorite, but the Wolverines pulled off the stunning 24–12 upset.

"You've got to understand, when I came here, I was sent to beat one and only one team," Schembechler said years later. "I only wanted Ohio State. That's the team I wanted to beat. I talked about it all the time. I did something every day to beat Ohio State and to beat Woody. That was the greatest challenge in my coaching career, was to beat him. If that added fuel to the fire, so be it. That's the way I approached it."

Schembechler's Michigan career was, of course, more than Michigan versus Ohio State. He was a seven-time Big Ten Coach of the Year, and he compiled a 194–48–5 record with the Wolverines from 1969 to 1989. In his 26 years as a head coach, he was 234–65–8 and never had a losing season. He was 11–9–1 overall against the Buckeyes.

There were other challenges throughout his career other than Hayes and the Buckeyes. Schembechler had a heart attack on the eve of his first Rose Bowl in 1970 and another in 1987. He had two quadruple-heart-bypass operations, and he also had diabetes.

He retired in 1989 because of his heart. His last game was a 17–10 loss to Southern California in the 1990 Rose Bowl. His final two teams in 1988 and 1989 won consecutive outright Big Ten titles.

Those Who Stay...

When Bo Schembechler arrived at Michigan in 1969, he knew there would be player defections. He intended to run hard, tough practices, and he wanted to build a challenging strength and conditioning program, and, rightfully, he assumed his style wouldn't be for everyone.

During his first training camp, Michigan started with about 140 players, but only 75 remained.

Schembechler's slogan would become: "Those who stay will be champions."

He created a sign with that slogan that has become forever linked with the Michigan program, and an updated version of that sign remains today in the locker room above the door. Schembechler's first sign, however, was defaced by John Prusiecki, who was one of the players who left the program. His final act was to take a marker and add a few more words to the sign.

"And those who leave will be doctors, lawyers, and captains of industry," Prusiecki scribbled.

His doctors later would say that Schembechler defied logic, beating the odds until his death at the age of 77. He died on the eve of the biggest Michigan–Ohio State game in history, when No. 1 OSU faced No. 2 Michigan in Ohio Stadium in 2006.

2 Michigan Stadium: The Biggest and the Best

The Big House.

These three simple words say it all about Michigan Stadium, one of the most widely recognized football facilities in the country.

Legendary Michigan football radio announcer Bob Ufer also said it all each Saturday when he announced to the listening audience that Michigan Stadium was the "hole that Yost dug, Crisler paid for, Canham carpeted, and Schembechler fills every cotton-pickin' Saturday afternoon."

Michigan Stadium has been the home of the Wolverines since 1927. Within its confines, fans have witnessed the Wolverines earn major victories. It has showcased national championship teams and Heisman Trophy winners. And it also, naturally, has been the site of some of Michigan's disappointments.

But Michigan fan or not, Michigan Stadium is a must-visit on a Saturday afternoon during the fall.

A recent $226 million renovation and expansion project gave the stadium a facelift. Unveiled in 2010, the stadium now sports 81 luxury boxes, a new press box, and more than 3,000 club seats. The total seating capacity is now 109,901, the highest capacity of any football stadium in the country. During the renovation in 2008 and 2009, Michigan Stadium's official capacity temporarily dipped from 107,501 to 106,201—ranking second behind Penn State's Beaver Stadium, capacity 107,282, for two seasons.

The Big House once again stands as the largest football stadium in the nation. But all of this would not be a reality had it not been for the vision of coach Fielding H. Yost.

In the early 1920s Yost began thinking large. Very large.

Even way back then, he envisioned a stadium that would seat 100,000 to 150,000 for each Michigan home game. But while campuses like Michigan State, Ohio State, and Illinois had built new stadiums during that era, Michigan had expanded its home, Ferry Field, and the regents were reluctant to approve another stadium enhancement, let alone new construction. Yost's plan was rejected, but he didn't give up. It eventually was approved on April 22, 1926.

His desire was to build the stadium where the Michigan Golf Course is now located, but that was nixed. Michigan Stadium would be built on land the university had purchased in 1925. That land, however, included an underground spring that

Stadium Mystery

For reasons that remain unknown, Fritz Crisler, in his role as athletics director, wanted the newly expanded Michigan Stadium that would be dedicated in 1956 to have a capacity figure that ended with "1".

The stadium that year had expanded from 97,239 to 101,001, thus beginning the tradition of ending all Michigan Stadium capacity numbers in that way.

In Michigan lore, that extra seat was later said to be reserved in honor of Crisler. The thing is, no one knows exactly where that seat is located.

had provided water to the school early on. The spring caused construction issues. Because of the high water table, nearly three-quarters of the stadium was built below ground level. Meanwhile, the surface was of a moist, sandy consistency, and legend has it that the quicksand-like ground engulfed a crane that remains under the stadium today.

Unheard of these days, construction of the new stadium would not be financed by taxpayers but by the sale of 3,000 $500 bonds. Those bonds entitled the holder to buy season tickets for every season from 1927 to 1936—because of the Great Depression, nothing was paid on the bonds between 1931 and 1936, and the bonds were not completely retired until the middle of October 1947.

Four hundred forty tons of reinforcing steel and 31,000 square feet of wire mesh were used in the construction of the 44-section, 72-row, 72,000-seat stadium at a cost of $950,000. Wisely, Yost designed Michigan Stadium to run north-south to keep the sun out of the players' eyes and to make wind less of an impact.

As the stadium neared completion just more than a year after the groundbreaking, Yost requested—and received—10,000 temporary seats for the concourse. With great foresight, he also had steel footings installed for a second deck. He had wanted to build a larger stadium, but to keep the construction costs down at the time, a "smaller" stadium was agreed upon. Still, knowing the steel footings were in place, Yost knew expansion was possible.

The stadium opened in 1927 at the corner of Main Street and Stadium Boulevard with a capacity of 84,401, the largest college-owned stadium in the country.

Michigan played Ohio Wesleyan in the first game at Michigan Stadium on October 1, 1927, and won 33–0. The stadium dedication came three weeks later against Ohio State. Michigan won that game 19–0, but more important, Michigan Stadium was sold out at $5 a ticket.

In the early 1930s electronic scoreboards were installed, making Michigan Stadium the first to feature that technology, and in 1949 Fritz Crisler, then the athletics director, had permanent metal seating replace the wood.

The field has undergone several facelifts. From 1927 to 1968, the field was natural grass. It was replaced in 1969 with the unforgiving TartanTurf—then thought to be an advantage for traction and wear and tear. It was changed back to grass in 1991, but because of the water table, maintaining a grass field became problematic. The field is now FieldTurf, a grass-like artificial surface.

3 The Story of the Helmet

So many Michigan players throughout the years have said one of the first reasons they became initially attracted to the program was because of the famed Michigan winged helmets. The blue helmet with the maize "wings" is easily one of the most recognizable in sports, if not *the* most recognizable. The design dates back to 1938, when Fritz Crisler arrived at Michigan from Princeton. Michigan's helmet had been black, and Crisler wanted to give the helmets distinction while making them useful at the same time.

Knowing his team would run the single-wing, noted for its speed and deception, Crisler wanted to make it easier for the Michigan players to locate each other on the field. He had the helmets painted in their now distinctive maize-and-blue winged pattern, the maize highlighting the original stitching of the leather helmets.

"There was a tendency to use different-colored helmets just for receivers in those days, but I always thought that would be as helpful for the defense as for the offense," Crisler had said.

Taking Flight

Coach Fritz Crisler brought the winged football helmet to Michigan, and it has become one of the most recognizable symbols of the program, but who said football players should be the only ones to wear wings?

Michigan hockey coach Red Berenson had for years wanted to incorporate the winged design into the team's helmets. On the eve of the 1989 CCHA playoffs, Berenson gave the Wolverines their winged hockey helmets.

Alex Roberts, a captain that season, said the players were walking up the stairs into the locker room when they started to smell fresh paint.

"We get up to the top of the stairs and see the training room tables in the hallway with a bunch of helmets on 'em painted dark blue with the yellow wings, just like the football team's," Roberts said in a *UM Press* article published in 2001. "We literally thought it was a joke. We're like, 'Where are our real helmets, the white ones?' Then Red comes in and says, 'You guys are wearing these.'"

The team that night bought their coach a baseball hat that features the football helmet design and presented it to him the following day. The players told him, "If we're gonna wear these things on our heads, you are, too."

Michigan's baseball and softball catchers and field hockey goalies wear helmets with the winged design. Swimmers also have worn racing caps with wings.

It essentially was the same basic helmet Crisler had introduced at Princeton in 1935.

Michigan's winged helmet made its debut in the 1938 season opener against Michigan State, a 14–0 Michigan victory. Sophomore halfback Paul Kromer scored two touchdowns, becoming the first Wolverine to score wearing the new-look helmet.

Certainly there are no tangible records that indicate the helmet had anything to do with the improved statistics, but in 1938 Michigan's total yardage was nearly double that in 1937, interceptions were cut nearly in half, and completion percentage increased by 9 percent. Could it have been the helmet?

All of that aside, the bottom line is Crisler's vision has made Michigan's helmet an undeniable symbol of the football program across the country.

"It's the most unique helmet in college football," said Erik Campbell, a former UM defensive back and assistant coach. "You don't have to put a name on it, or a logo on it…people know exactly what school it's from."

As a kid, Doug Skene, a former Michigan offensive lineman, wanted only one thing for Christmas—a Michigan helmet. He asked for the helmet several years in a row. "[I wanted it] to wear when I played Nerf football with Greg, Matt, Jeff, and Corey, friends from the old neighborhood," Skene said. "I was going to be Leach or Carter in the backyard."

Santa never left Skene the helmet. "I had to earn it myself," he said. "My dad told me when I was in middle school that if I *really* wanted to play at Michigan, I had to be the best. That helmet wasn't going to be a Christmas gift given to me by anyone.

"After I shook Bo's hand and agreed to come to Michigan in that summer of 1987, I couldn't wait to get that helmet! When I stepped on that practice field for the first time with my classmates and saw all of us in our helmets, my eyes welled up."

Skene's 11-year-old son in 2008 asked for a Michigan helmet for Christmas. He was told that he would have to earn it, just as his father and all of the Michigan players had.

"Mine sits in my office today, and I'll have it until I die," Skene said.

4 The Game: The Michigan–Ohio State Rivalry

In so many ways, how Michigan players are defined has as much to do with that team down south in Columbus as how Ohio State players are defined by that school up north.

It is difficult to mention one without the other. Michigan–Ohio State, Ohio State–Michigan. It was rated the No. 1 rivalry in sports by ESPN, and it is unlikely that any who follow either team would argue with that assessment.

"Every time they play, one team can beat the other," the late, legendary Michigan coach Bo Schembechler said. "I don't care if one has had a better year than the other—it doesn't make any difference. Anything can happen. It's always been that kind of a game, and that's probably caught the eye of the nation."

To be sure, when Michigan and Ohio State play in late November in the regular-season finale for both schools, the nation watches.

The rivalry has a rich history that dates back to 1897. "The Game," as most refer to it, has more often than not had plenty riding on it. It frequently determined the Big Ten Conference champion and sealed bowl destinations—after, of course, the Big Ten released its conference teams to play in more than just the Rose Bowl. It has wrecked national-championship hopes and helped fulfill national-title dreams.

Ask players and coaches from both sides of the rivalry, and they will assert that the Michigan–Ohio State game defined their college careers.

"You ask the guys, 'How many times did you beat Ohio State?'" Schembechler once said. "If you want to be recognized around [Ann Arbor] as a coach or a player, you beat Ohio State. That's what you're here for. I'm sure that's exactly what they say down there."

But the rivalry didn't start with a bang. Michigan held a 13–0–2 record in the first 15 years of the matchup before the Chic Harley–led Buckeyes finally won in 1919, 13–3, at Ann Arbor.

Since 1918, the game has alternated between Columbus and Ann Arbor, with Michigan hosting The Game in odd years. It has been played at vaunted Ohio Stadium since 1922 and at Michigan's Big House, Michigan Stadium, since 1927.

The Game truly became The Game during the well-known "10-Year War," the series of 10 games from 1969 to 1978 between Ohio State's Woody Hayes and Michigan's Bo Schembechler. They both were fiery and driven, and as an added enhancement to the rivalry, Schembechler had played for Hayes at Miami (Ohio) and coached under him at OSU.

Give them credit for making their first Michigan–Ohio State meeting breathtaking, stunning, and memorable. It was the game that put the 10-Year War in action and captivated the country. Ohio State, ranked No. 1 and clearly the nation's best team, had won 22 straight. Michigan was 7–2 under its new coach. The Wolverines intercepted Ohio State six times en route to the 24–12 upset. The Michigan players carried Schembechler on their shoulders.

Four times between 1970 and 1975, Michigan and Ohio State were each ranked in the top five of the AP poll before meeting. During the 10-Year War, the teams shared the Big Ten title six times. Schembechler was 5–4–1 against Hayes.

10 Years of War

For 10 years, the old friends were bitter rivals. Michigan coach Bo Schembechler had played for and coached under Ohio State coach Woody Hayes. But when Schembechler arrived at Michigan in 1969, there was nothing the two men wanted more each year than to beat the other.

"I know for a fact that Woody was kind of surprised when I was named coach here," Schembechler said. "Whether people realized it or not, that was going to add a little something to the rivalry."

Their intense rivalry spanned a decade and is known as the "10-Year War." Michigan and Ohio State dominated the Big Ten during those years, and the two teams shared the Big Ten title six times.

When the war had ended, Schembechler had the slight advantage, with a series record of 5–4–1.

"They've always been very intense and everything, but I must admit, I probably enjoyed the 10 years with Woody more than any of the other games that I played against Ohio State," Schembechler said. Here's how the games played out:

Date	Score	Location
11-22-69	UM 24–12	Michigan Stadium
11-21-70	OSU 20–9	Ohio Stadium
11-20-71	UM 10–7	Michigan Stadium
11-25-72	OSU 14–11	Ohio Stadium
11-24-73	10–10	Michigan Stadium
11-23-74	OSU 12–10	Ohio Stadium
11-22-75	OSU 21–14	Michigan Stadium
11-20-76	UM 22–0	Ohio Stadium
11-19-77	UM 14–6	Michigan Stadium
11-25-78	UM 14–3	Ohio Stadium

Of course, The Game didn't stop being The Game at the conclusion of those 10 meetings. Earle Bruce became the next head coach of the Buckeyes and held a 5–4 record against Schembechler's teams. Bruce was fired just before the 1987 game, but he was allowed to coach his final Michigan game. Inspired by their coach's firing, the Buckeyes pulled off the 23–20 upset.

The John Cooper era began at Ohio State in 1988. He had some absolutely fine, national-championship-caliber teams, particularly those in 1993, 1995, and 1996, when the Buckeyes entered The Game unbeaten. Cooper, who began his Michigan–Ohio State career facing Schembechler and then Gary Moeller starting in 1990 and Lloyd Carr beginning in 1995, had a disappointing 2–10–1 record against the Wolverines. It wasn't pretty for Cooper's Buckeyes. They entered the 1993 game with a 9–0–1 record and had a shot at an outright Big Ten title. Michigan won 28–0.

"If you'd told me we would come up here and get beat 28–0, I'd have probably stayed home," Cooper said.

Two years later, the Buckeyes were ranked No. 2 when they entered the game in Ann Arbor against the No. 18 Wolverines. The Wolverines, however, had been given locker-room material courtesy of the Buckeyes' Terry Glenn, who said during a television interview that, "Michigan's nothing." Michigan running back Tim Biakabutuka showed the Buckeyes plenty of something when he rushed for 313 yards in the Wolverines' 31–23 upset.

The Buckeyes had high hopes in 1996 entering the Michigan game. Again, they were ranked No. 2 nationally and were 10–0. They led 9–0 at halftime, but after Brian Griese took over at quarterback for injured Scott Dreisbach, he hit Tai Streets on a touchdown pass that sparked Michigan's 13–9 victory.

With everything on the line in 1997 for the Wolverines, it was No. 1 Michigan against No. 4 Ohio State. Michigan was playing for a perfect regular season while trying to maintain its national-title hopes. The Wolverines, sparked by eventual Heisman Trophy–winner Charles Woodson, won 20–14.

Ohio State has had the clear edge over Michigan in the early part of this century, thanks to coach Jim Tressel, who took over from Cooper in 2001. Tressel made clear to Buckeyes fans his intention as the OSU football coach. He was introduced during halftime of a basketball game against Michigan that January, and emphasized his goal.

"I can assure you that you will be proud of our young people in the classroom, in the community, and most especially in 310 days in Ann Arbor, Michigan, on the football field," Tressel said before being showered by applause.

For coaches and players alike, Michigan–Ohio State, Ohio State–Michigan, means everything.

"This is the pressure game," Schembechler said. "This is the big one. Just like at Ohio State, they always know your record against Michigan. Here, they always know the coach's record against Ohio State. That's the way it is. That's what makes it such a beautiful rivalry. I don't know that there's another one in the country that is as intense and is as great a rivalry as this one."

5 1969: The 10-Year War Begins

Former Michigan tight end Jim Mandich has been quoted as saying it is impossible to talk about the 1969 Michigan–Ohio State game without talking about the 1968 game at Ohio Stadium.

The Wolverines had been humiliated in that game, losing 50–14, but the biggest slap had been coach Woody Hayes' decision to go for a two-point conversion after the final score.

Bo Schembechler was not on Michigan's sideline that season coaching the Wolverines. But when he arrived in Ann Arbor in 1969, beating Ohio State—and his mentor, Hayes, for whom he had played at Miami (Ohio) and coached under at OSU—was his primary goal. To that end, Schembechler was committed to motivating the Wolverines in any way.

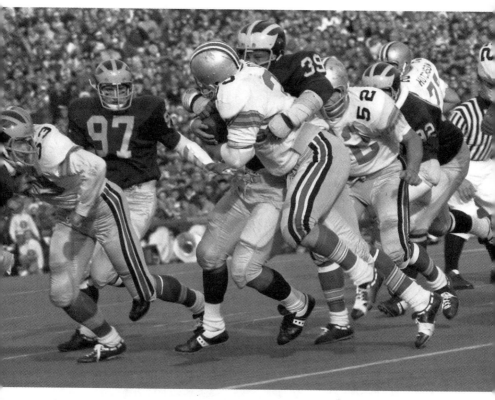

The 1969 game against Ohio State started the fabled "10-Year War." Photo courtesy Bentley Historical Library, University of Michigan.

He had the number 50, representing the number of points the Buckeyes had scored the year before, displayed everywhere. It was in the locker room, and it was taped to the practice uniforms and to the helmets of the scout team.

Michigan and Schembechler faced a daunting task that November in Michigan Stadium, which set a then-record 103,588 for the final regular-season game. Ohio State had won the national championship in 1968, had won 22 straight games, was ranked No. 1 in the country, and was, by all accounts, an absolutely tremendous, weakness-free team.

The Wolverines were 17-point underdogs. They didn't realize that Schembechler had been preparing the team for Ohio State all

"Only the Good Ones..."

Ohioans don't think kindly of their native-born sons who decide to leave the Buckeye state and head to "that school up north," as legendary OSU coach Woody Hayes used to refer to Michigan. But over the years, Michigan's football roster has been dotted with young men from Ohio, some of whom went on to greatness wearing the maize and blue.

Two of the Wolverines' three Heisman Trophy winners—Charles Woodson and Desmond Howard—are from Ohio. Some of the others included John Kolesar, Jim Mandich, Elvis Grbac, Dan Dierdorf, Tom Curtis, Bob Chappuis, and Marcus Ray, who grew up in Columbus.

Kolesar was a major thorn in the sides of all Buckeyes in 1988. He accounted for 100 yards on two plays, including an unbelievable leaping catch in double coverage at the goal line. Kolesar was magical in Michigan's 34–31 victory at Ohio Stadium.

That's not exactly the way to make friends in Ohio, where Kolesar lives, but he grew used to the tensions. His father, William, also played at Michigan. Even today, John Kolesar said he gets verbally harassed by Buckeye fans.

"But in a good way," Kolesar (1985–1988) said. "They call me a bad word, and then they buy me a beer. They felt proud of me because here's a friend they grew up with, but in the other sense, they're real loyal Ohio State fans. And Ohio State loyalty is very strong."

Dennis Franklin, a Michigan quarterback (1972–1974) from Massillon, Ohio, drove the knife in deep. Although he insists his quote was taken slightly out of context, what appeared in the newspaper lived on in the Ohio State locker room. Franklin had been asked about being an Ohioan and playing for Michigan and he said, "Only the good ones" from Ohio go to Michigan.

He later claimed he said, "*Some* of the good ones."

It didn't matter.

The Buckeyes had that quote on their bulletin board for years.

Bruce Ruhl, one of the rare Michigan natives who ventured south to play for Ohio State, said he learned in 1973 as a freshman about the Franklin quote.

"I saw this statement on the bulletin board my freshman year, 'Only the good ones, only the good ones,' and no one could explain what that meant," Ruhl said. "Until the week before the Michigan game when in our lockers there was a picture of Dennis Franklin and his quote."

16

season, practicing something each day that would be used in late November.

On the eve of the '69 game, Schembechler told reporters he was about to "fight my football father."

Hayes decided to practice some gamesmanship the day of the game and had the Buckeyes warming up on Michigan's side of the field. Schembechler led his team out to the field, then walked up to Hayes and said, "Coach, you are warming up on the wrong side of the field." Hayes motioned his players to the other side, but the Wolverines were fired up by the proceedings.

"I remember in 1969, they told me our team was going to get too high early in the week," Schembechler later said. "I said, 'Nah, let's just let them get higher.' I don't think they can get too high."

Michigan held a 14–12 first-half lead when Barry Pierson gave the Wolverines an enormous boost. He returned the punt from Mike Sensibaugh to the OSU 3-yard line. Michigan scored two plays later to take a 21–12 lead. The Wolverines led 24–12 at halftime.

Pierson had three interceptions in the second half, and Tom Curtis added two to lead the Michigan defense. The Buckeyes committed seven turnovers, including six interceptions.

Schembechler was carried off the field by his players, and the Michigan Stadium crowd went crazy. Michigan won the Big Ten title and the trip to the Rose Bowl.

"It put our program on the map," Schembechler said of the win. "I mean, 'Schembechler' wasn't exactly a household name in those days."

Former Michigan coach and athletics director Fritz Crisler watched the game from his hospital bed and later wrote Schembechler to tell him how proud he was to be a Michigan Man after watching that performance.

It was the game that defined the Michigan–Ohio State rivalry and kicked off the 10-Year War between Woody and Bo, and it was Schembechler's greatest victory.

"It was Woody's greatest team, he admitted that," Schembechler said. "We beat them here. It was my first year, and I'm just trying to establish myself as a coach here. I think the fact that we were able to win that game really set the tone here for my program.

"I wanted to establish a tough program. I didn't want to hear any more of that whispering out there that Michigan was talented but not tough. That never happened again. I wasn't going to let it. I put them through a lot of hell [that season]. Those that stayed won the championship."

6 The Game 2006: No. 1 OSU vs. No. 2 Michigan

On so many levels, the 2006 Michigan–Ohio State game was memorable.

Sadly, legendary Michigan coach Bo Schembechler, who made a name for himself by beating then–No. 1 Ohio State in 1969 in his first season with the Wolverines, passed away on the eve of The Game. Schembechler was 77.

Remarkably, it was the first No. 1 versus No. 2 matchup in the storied rivalry.

The game lived up to its billing and the incredible hype that week and was a fitting tribute to Schembechler, the Ohio-native who coached at "that school up north."

On the Monday morning of game week, Schembechler spoke to the media, including representatives from the Columbus press, about the Michigan–Ohio State rivalry and the upcoming game, in particular.

"This game is something special," said Schembechler, who, at coach Lloyd Carr's request, spoke to the team mid-week. "If you

A Legend Dies

Bo Schembechler passed away on the eve of the biggest game in the history of the rivalry he loved the most and defined his career. Schembechler was 77 in 2006 when his heart gave way after he collapsed at the studios of WXYZ-TV in the Detroit suburb of Southfield. He was there to tape his weekly college football show.

The next day, No. 1 Ohio State faced No. 2 Michigan at Ohio State in a game that had been hyped nationally all week. In fact, Schembechler appeared before media covering the two football programs five days before the game.

He suffered his first heart attack on the eve of his first Rose Bowl in 1970 and endured another one in 1987. He had two quadruple-heart-bypass operations and also had diabetes.

Ohio State paid homage to Schembechler in a video tribute shown on the scoreboard before kickoff. The crowd of 105,708 cheered respectfully.

"Michigan has lost a coach and patriarch," the public-address announcer said. "The Big Ten has lost a legend and icon. Ohio State has lost an alumnus and friend."

The Wolverines, coached by Lloyd Carr—a man who considered Schembechler a dear friend—lost that game. Earlier in the week, Carr visited Schembechler in his office at Schembechler Hall and asked him to speak to the team the Thursday night before the game. Schembechler did so.

"It was definitely difficult for us," UM quarterback Chad Henne said. "Coach Carr loves him dearly and so do we. It's sad to see him go. We tried to fight for him today."

total up the Big Ten championships, it's usually one or the other. But we never went into this game ranked No. 1 and 2 in the nation. This is a first. It's pretty clear-cut that everybody feels that these are the two best teams in the nation.

"I don't think there will be a football game played this year with so many gifted athletes on the field. I just don't see one any bigger than this. I see this game as being a great classic."

Schembechler was prophetic—this one was a classic. Both teams entered the annual rivalry game with top-notch defenses. But this game would be about the offenses, as top-ranked Ohio State, led by quarterback Troy Smith, who had had incredible success against the Wolverines, won 42–39.

"I thought it would be a low-scoring game," said Michigan's defensive end LaMarr Woodley, who had 11 sacks in 11 games but couldn't record one against the Buckeyes. "It kind of shocked everybody."

Ohio State finished the season 12–0 with an outright Big Ten championship for the first time since 1984 and a spot in the national title game. Michigan, meanwhile, finished 11–1 overall, and even after the loss was still a potential Buckeyes opponent for the national championship.

The Michigan and Ohio State defenses entered the game yielding an average 20 points a game. Clearly, they were unable to stop each other. This was the second-highest-scoring game in the series, which dates back to 1897, but it was the highest-scoring game in the modern era. Michigan won 86–0 in the 1902 game, the most points scored in the rivalry.

Try as they may, the Wolverines could not stop Troy Smith, who clinched the Heisman Trophy with his performance in that game. He was 29-of-41 for 316 yards and four touchdowns.

"This is The Ohio State University–Michigan game," Smith said after the game. "It's the biggest game in college football. And today, the best team won."

It took everything for the Buckeyes to win, though. They twice led by 14 points, but the Wolverines, who were led by Mike Hart's 142 yards and three touchdowns, would not go away.

Unfortunately for the Wolverines, there was a critical, game-changing defensive play with six minutes to go. They appeared on the verge of forcing an Ohio State punt when junior linebacker Shawn Crable was called for roughing the quarterback when he hit Smith as he headed out of bounds. The play gave Ohio State a fresh set of downs. The Buckeyes took advantage, and Smith hit Brian Robiskie for a touchdown to build a 42–31 lead.

Michigan, again, would not go away. With 2:16 left in the game, Chad Henne completed a 16-yard touchdown pass to tight end Tyler Ecker. Steve Breaston scored on a two-point conversion to cut the deficit to 42–39. The Wolverines' ensuing onside kick, however, was caught by OSU's Ted Ginn Jr. to essentially end the game.

An average 14.5 million households tuned into the Michigan–Ohio State game, making it then the most-watched college football game since 1992.

Even after the Michigan loss, there was heated debate as to whether the Wolverines should face the Buckeyes in a rematch in the national championship game. Ultimately, Florida reached the game.

7 Fielding H. Yost: Stadium Builder

Examine Michigan football tradition and sit in Michigan Stadium, and you can't help but *feel* the presence of Fielding H. Yost.

Yost was the brilliant coach who took over the program in 1901 and put his stamp everywhere. He was a dynamic visionary who loved "Meeshegan," as he called it, and wanted nothing more than to make it the premier football program with the biggest stadium.

He was the architect of some of the most dominating teams in the history of football, the "point-a-minute" teams of the early 1900s that seemingly scored at will during a five-year run. Those teams, from 1901 through 1905, outscored their opponents 2,821–42, and went 55–1–1. A 2–0 loss at Chicago in the 1905 season-ender and a 6–6 tie at Minnesota in 1903—the game that sparked the Little Brown Jug trophy game—were the only blemishes.

Yost coached Michigan for 25 years, during which he compiled a 165–29–10 record, and he served as athletics director for 20 years.

The West Virginia native, who received a law degree from West Virginia University, began his coaching career at Ohio Wesleyan, then coached briefly at Kansas and Nebraska. In 1900 he became the head coach at Stanford, a post he held for a year before the school enacted a rule that only Stanford graduates could coach its football team.

In his first season in 1901, Yost, who reportedly said upon arrival in Ann Arbor that "Michigan isn't going to lose a game," led the Wolverines to an 11–0 record and defeated Stanford 49–0 in the inaugural Rose Bowl. They did not yield a point that season—and scored 550 points—and won the national championship, the first of four straight championships.

He was a noted stickler for preparation and once said, "Many have the will to win, but few have the will to prepare." His practices were, of course, organized and disciplined, and he constantly yelled, "Hurry up! Hurry up!" thus earning the nickname "Hurry Up" Yost.

His brilliance as a football coach cannot be denied. His point-a-minute teams were legendary, and his innovations, such as the creation of the linebacker position, changed the game. But coaching was not Yost's only contribution to Michigan. He served well as its athletics director from 1921 to 1941. It was his vision that resulted in the construction of Michigan Stadium, not to mention Yost Field House (now known as Yost Ice Arena), the Michigan Golf Course—designed by Alistair MacKenzie—and the nation's first intramural sports building.

Michigan Stadium is Yost's lasting legacy. In the early 1920s, the era in which so many schools were building stadiums, Yost campaigned for a stadium that would replace 42,000-seat Ferry Field. He knew the odds were slim since Ferry Field had just been expanded, and the regents were not inclined to make this approval.

Yost, who was stubborn and charming, eventually got his way. The stadium construction was approved on April 22, 1926, and in the fall of 1927 Michigan Stadium, seating 84,401 and costing just less than $1 million, was christened at the corner of Main Street and Stadium Boulevard.

After the dedication game against Ohio State, a 21–0 victory by the Wolverines, Yost walked back from the stadium to the campus with Bennie Oosterbaan, the star of that 1927 team and a future Michigan coach. Oosterbaan told the *Ann Arbor Observer* that Yost was in great spirits after that victory.

"We'd won, and the stadium was completely filled," Oosterbaan told the publication. "He turned to me and said, 'Bennie, do you know what the best thing about that new stadium is? Eighty-five thousand people paid $5 apiece for their seats, and Bennie, they had to leave the seats there!'"

Yost was 75 when he died on October 20, 1946, in Ann Arbor.

"No other man has ever given as much heart, soul, brains, and tongue to the game he loved—football," famed sportswriter Grantland Rice once said of Yost.

Michigan fans would be hard-pressed to disagree.

8 Fritz Crisler: Team Builder

Herbert Orin "Fritz" Crisler was an innovator who changed college football while shaping Michigan along the way. During his glory years at Michigan, from 1938 to 1947—highlight that last season with a national championship—Crisler created two-platoon football, which defined the college and pro game as we now know it, and he brought to Michigan what would become

Crisler the Creator

World War II had affected the United States in multiple ways, and college football was not immune. In 1944 a conference rule was changed, and freshmen were allowed to play with the varsity. Even so, Michigan coach Fritz Crisler entered the 1945 season with a young team of inexperienced 17-year-olds.

The Wolverines, who started six freshmen, were preparing to face an indestructible Army team in the fifth game of the season. The Cadets were led by seasoned 23-year-olds who had served their time overseas and had returned to college. Army, led by Doc Blanchard and Glenn Davis, were bigger, stronger, and more experienced.

Crisler knew Michigan stood little chance against Army. But he also noticed a loophole in the substitution rule that had been changed in 1941 in anticipation of the effect the war would have on college football. The rule specifically allowed a player to sub into the game "at any time" instead of once a quarter. "Those three little words changed the game," Crisler later said.

Crisler created what became known as two-platoon football out of necessity, and it would forever change the game. He divided the Wolverines into offensive and defensive specialists two weeks before the Army game.

"The rules had been so liberalized during the war so coaches could substitute freely with as many men as they wanted to," Crisler said in an interview in 1968. "It suddenly occurred to me that if we could use any boy whenever we wanted, why not look for the best ball carriers, passers, and receivers and put the best blockers up front ahead of them, then take them out when the ball changed hands and throw in the best tacklers and pass defenders."

Two-platoon football allowed for the evolution of the T formation because the quarterback could specialize on offense.

perhaps the most recognizable symbol in college football—the famed maize-and-blue winged helmet.

Crisler was a commanding presence. He was not exactly warm to his players or popular, for that matter, but they respected him. His players jokingly referred to him as "The Lord" and even a half-century after playing for Crisler, they thought of him that way, always with profound respect and even deeper admiration.

During his 10 seasons with the Wolverines, Crisler's teams went 71–16–3, including the perfect season in 1947 and the crowning national championship. Crisler-coached teams were never out of the top-20 rankings, and in eight of those 10 seasons, the Wolverines were ranked ninth or better.

Crisler arrived at Michigan from Princeton following four dismal seasons during which the Wolverines went 10–22 overall, including two 1–7 seasons.

"There is no doubt about it, Michigan is in a terrible mess," Crisler wrote to Amos Alonzo Stagg, his coach at Chicago.

Despite the mess, Crisler inherited two special sophomores, Tom Harmon and Forest Evashevski. He established himself quickly, making appearances around town, trying to drum up support. He brought with him from Princeton the tear-away jerseys he had conceived, and he created the winged helmet, painted to help passers locate receivers downfield.

That first season, 1938, Crisler's Wolverines went 6–1–1 and finished second in the Big Ten, but they defeated Michigan State, which they had not done the four previous meetings. Michigan outscored is opponents 131–40 that season, a huge turnaround considering the Wolverines had been outscored 110–54 the year before.

Harmon truly was a gift for Crisler. He was a triple-threat who could run, pass, and punt. Harmon, coupled with Crisler's tough, daily two-hour workouts and intuitive feel for the game, turned around the Wolverines.

In 1940, Crisler's third season, the Wolverines went 7–1 and finished ranked third nationally. During the first three games, Harmon scored 69 points. He appeared on the cover of *Life* magazine and won the Heisman Trophy.

And at that stage in his career, Crisler was gaining recognition.

"No one could utilize the available talent like Crisler," an unidentified rival coach once said. "Players sometimes said they didn't like him because he was stern, aloof, and driven. But they would die for him on the football field."

With Harmon gone, Crisler had to, in a sense, rebuild. Team captain Bob Westfall later said that his coach's "revitalizing and reshaping" of the 1941 team "was possibly Crisler's finest hour."

Michigan went 6–1–1 that season and was ranked No. 5 nationally. Crisler's Wolverines won a Big Ten championship in 1943, but his greatest success came in 1947.

He faced interesting post–World War II issues. There was an unusual mix of younger players and men who had returned from the war and re-enrolled in school. Crisler's other challenge that year was the size of his team—overall, the Wolverines were fairly small, with the largest player weighing 220 pounds. The players on the offensive line averaged 182 pounds.

The creative Crisler went with the single-wing, an offense in which size did not matter—this was all about skill, quickness, and ballhandling. There were 170 plays in the Michigan playbook, and there was a madcap combination of double-reverses, criss-crosses, and spins. Ninety percent of the plays Crisler devised had at least one exchange and, frequently, as many as three, sometimes more.

"It was fun to play that system," said Bob Chappuis.

The national press was so awed by Michigan, the Wolverines were dubbed the "Mad Magicians." They went 10–0 and outscored opponents 394–53. The Wolverines shut out USC 49–0 in the Rose Bowl, and with that win, the Associated Press, in an unprecedented move, conducted another poll. Writers were asked to vote for either Michigan (10–0) or Notre Dame (9–0). The poll was revealed January 6, and Michigan won the national championship with 226 first-place votes to Notre Dame's 119.

Twenty-five years later Crisler attended a team reunion despite an illness, but he did not speak. Instead, he wrote each player a sentimental letter. The players were stunned that their old coach, never one for sentiment, expressed his emotions.

"There are times when the heart is too full for utterance," he wrote. "Being with you on the 25th anniversary was one of those times."

Crisler served as Michigan's athletics director for 27 years until 1968, and under his watch, Michigan Stadium twice was expanded, to 101,001 by the time his tenure had ended.

9 Brady Hoke: A New Era

Brady Hoke said he would have walked from his previous job in San Diego to Ann Arbor if that's what was needed to become the head coach at Michigan.

It was a job he had always coveted, from the time he was a defensive assistant with the Wolverines and even while he was head coach at Ball State and San Diego State.

When Hoke, then 52 years old, was hired on January 11, 2011, as Michigan's 19th head coach, replacing Rich Rodriguez, he fulfilled his dream. He signed a six-year contract.

Former Michigan coach Lloyd Carr, for whom Hoke worked eight seasons as a defensive assistant (1995 to 2002), would sit down with each of his assistants at the conclusion of every season and asked what they wanted from coaching.

"I'll never forget, one year I'm interviewing Brady and he says, 'I want to be the head coach at the University of Michigan,'" Carr said. "I couldn't help but think about that [when Hoke was hired], because it was a dream for him."

Hoke left Michigan to become head coach at Ball State, his alma mater. He was there from 2003 to 2008, including a 12–1 record in 2008, and then left for San Diego State, where he spent two seasons. He was 47–50 overall as a head coach when he arrived at Michigan.

He took a team that had gone 15–22 the previous three seasons and led the Wolverines to an 11–2 record, including a Sugar Bowl victory, and he snapped the team's seven-game losing streak to archrival Ohio State.

But even before the Wolverines took the field, Hoke won over the fan base during his first news conference formally introducing him as head coach.

Hoke grew up near Dayton, Ohio, and he has said by the time he was about 12 years old, he was a contrarian—while his friends

Brady Hoke encourages his players during Michigan's October 2011 win over Minnesota in Ann Arbor. In his first season as head coach, the former Lloyd Carr assistant led the Wolverines to an 11–2 record—including Michigan's first win over Ohio State since 2003.

were Ohio State fans, he rooted for Michigan. He has a clear understanding of The Game, the Michigan–Ohio State game, and what it means for both fan bases and college football.

In that first news conference, Hoke made it readily apparent from the start he gets the rivalry.

He pounded the lectern when he said the Ohio State game "is the most important game on that schedule. It's almost personal."

Actually, he never said the word "State" and won't. He refers to the Buckeyes only as "Ohio," and that is how the Buckeyes are represented on the schedule in the Wolverines' team meeting room.

While Hoke's understanding of The Game came through loud and clear, he might have scored even more points with Michigan fans when he was asked by a reporter about the state of the program. Because of the slide the previous three years that included only one bowl appearance and no consistent presence in the Top 25 polls, there had been some talk that the Michigan program had lost its relevance nationally.

Hoke was taken aback.

"This is an elite job and will continue to be an elite job," he said. "This is Michigan, for God's sake."

That is a phrase that has been frequently quoted by fans doing their best Hoke impersonations, although it isn't easy to replicate his distinctive rasp. The "This is Michigan" portion of the phrase was used in posters, schedule cards, and items of that nature during the 2011 season.

Shortly after taking the Michigan job, Hoke assembled his staff that includes defensive coordinator Greg Mattison, who left the same position with the NFL's Baltimore Ravens. By the end of the 2011 season, Mattison had taken a Michigan defense that had been among the nation's worst in 2010 and molded it into one of the country's best. Hoke brought with him from San Diego State several of his assistants, including offensive coordinator Al Borges.

Among Hoke's many jobs his first season was mending some of the fences that had splintered in the Michigan football family. During the Rodriguez Era, there was evidence that former players had disagreements with the way a number of things were handled, and occasionally those differences were aired publicly.

Michigan athletic director Dave Brandon hoped that with this hire, the Michigan family would be reunited.

"I made it real clear one of the biggest challenges was to bring Michigan back together," Brandon said. "One of the strengths of Michigan has been our united front and our support for one another.

"We had that coach after coach, but we really went through a three-year period of time we were divided, at odds, finger pointing. We all learned that's not a good place to be if you want to win, if you want a program to be proud of. The objective and hope was to find a way to bring everyone back and be united around the program. We've taken huge strides in that direction and credit Brady Hoke and his staff."

10 1997: Perfection and a National Title

Twelve games. Twelve victories. Perfection.

Led by a former walk-on quarterback, a Heisman Trophy–winning cornerback, a stingy defense, and a steady offense, Michigan's magical 1997 season culminated with a victory over Washington State in the Rose Bowl, and a share of the national championship.

For coach Lloyd Carr, this was his legacy-making season.

"What a special group of people it was," Carr said a decade after the championship, Michigan's first since 1948.

At the time, the Wolverines appreciated every practice, every test, every win. Looking back, they appreciate it even more.

"You look back on it, and you just realized how special it is," said Steve Hutchinson, who started at left guard. "I've played in the Super Bowl, but to be able to not lose a game—to go out 12 weeks in a row and not lose a game—is special."

There were plenty of defining moments that season, but one game in particular stood out as the hinge game. Against Iowa on October 18, the sixth game of the season, the Wolverines made mistakes. Quarterback Brian Griese, a former walk-on who had returned for his fifth season, threw three interceptions, the Wolverines had a punt blocked, and they allowed touchdowns of 53 and 61 yards in the first half to trail 21–7 at home.

Michigan didn't panic, and Griese proved his mettle in the second half, directing a 28–24 comeback victory. He completed a two-yard pass to tight end Jerame Tuman with 2:55 left for the win.

"The Iowa game was a pivotal game for me, obviously, but also, I think, for the team," Griese said. "From that point on, we always felt like we were going to find a way to win. That was kind of the theme after that game for myself and everybody else that no matter how bad it got during the course of the rest of the year, we always knew if we stuck together we'd find a way to win."

Three weeks later, Michigan elevated its game and itself in the national spotlight. Penn State was riding a 12-game winning streak and was ranked No. 3, while unbeaten Michigan was No. 4. The Nittany Lions were averaging 464.6 yards of offense and had the advantage of hosting the game at Beaver Stadium. Michigan overwhelmed Penn State, annihilating the Nittany Lions 34–8. The Wolverines held the Penn State offense in check with 169 total yards, including just 38 in the first half. Meanwhile, on that same day, top-ranked Nebraska had to go into overtime to beat Missouri. By the next Monday, Michigan was ranked No. 1.

The Michigan Band: Creator of "Script Ohio"

Let's settle this from the start—the Michigan marching band did it first. In 1932 at Ohio Stadium the Michigan band stood in a formation that spelled out "Ohio" in script form while the band played the OSU fight song, "Fight the Team."

And this absolutely may have been the source for the Ohio State marching band's "Script Ohio," which, unlike Michigan's stationary formation in 1932, is an animated formation. Ohio State took the original and added movement as the band members follow the lead of the drum major.

Ohio State's "Script Ohio" tradition began four years after Michigan first spelled "Ohio" in script. It evolved into a revolving block "O" and the famous dotting of the "i" by the sousaphone player.

So if you want to irritate Buckeye fans, remind them that the origins, simple though they may have been, of "Script Ohio" were rooted in the Michigan marching band.

"Late in that game, I knew we had a chance to do something really special, because we played as well as we could have played," Carr said. "If you're doing that, that late in the season, you have a chance."

The Wolverines went on the road the following week, and in frigid playing conditions defeated Wisconsin 26–16.

That left...Ohio State.

How many times had Michigan played spoiler for the Buckeyes in the 1990s? This was Ohio State's chance. But Charles Woodson, dynamic all season, playing at cornerback and also on offense and in the kick-return game, sealed the Heisman Trophy with his performance in a tight 20–14 victory.

Woodson returned a punt for a touchdown, intercepted a pass in the end zone, caught a 37-yard pass that set up a score, broke up one pass, and had three tackles.

On to the Rose Bowl, Carr's favorite college football venue, aside from Michigan Stadium. The Wolverines were feeling good, and they were confident.

"By the time we got to the Rose Bowl, I wouldn't say we were cocky, but it was almost to the point we had played for each other all year long, it was inevitable," Hutchinson said.

Michigan completed its magical season with a 21–16 victory over the Ryan Leaf–led Washington State Cougars. Griese was named MVP of the Rose Bowl, and Carr had etched his name in Michigan history.

The Wolverines, however, shared the national championship with Nebraska, and both were honored together that spring at the White House. Michigan finished first in the AP writers' poll, and Nebraska was second; in the *USA Today*/Coaches' poll, Nebraska finished first, and Michigan second.

11 Denard Robinson: Shoelace

Think Denard Robinson, you think No. 16, dreadlocks, a mega-watt smile, and blazing speed.

Oh, and untied shoelaces.

Velcro keeps his cleats on his feet, but the laces? They're untied, hence his well-recognized nickname, "Shoelace".

Robinson, from Deerfield Beach, Florida, began his career as the Wolverines' starting quarterback as a sophomore in 2010. He turned heads with his elusive style and speed that season, setting a single-season NCAA rushing record for a quarterback with 1,702 yards. Also that season, he became the first player in NCAA history to throw for 2,500 yards and rush for 1,500 in a single season.

He was voted Big Ten Offensive Player of the Year that season.

But following the 2010 season, head coach Rich Rodriguez, who recruited Robinson to run his spread offense, was fired. Brady

Denard Robinson rushes for a 41-yard touchdown during Michigan's 2011 win over Ohio State. The quarterback known as "Shoelace" set a single-season NCAA rushing record for a quarterback with 1,702 yards in 2010.

Hoke became head coach in early 2011 and with him came offensive coordinator Al Borges, a pro-style guru.

Borges wasn't going to try to shape Robinson into Tom Brady, but both men would have to make compromises. Borges had no interest in holding Robinson back as a runner, since, after all, his feet had made the difference in many games for the Wolverines.

But Borges' objective upon arrival was to add pro-style elements to Robinson's game, while keeping some of the spread, and the ultimate goal was to keep Robinson healthy.

"I told him from the beginning, from day one, that he wasn't going to rush for 70, 80 yards, because we're going to keep him in one piece if it killed us," Borges said. "He has accepted his role in this offense, which is always huge, always huge, but certain phases of what he had done before are not quite as prominent now. And that would be easy for a kid to say, 'What the heck?'

"Not him. He's been a pleasure to coach."

Robinson, in his second full season as a starter in 2011, helped lead the Wolverines to an 11–2 record, including a victory in the Sugar Bowl. His rushing numbers did decline a bit—down to 1,176—but cutting back Robinson's number of carries while finding a primary back who could share the rushing load was always the objective.

Still, Robinson became the fourth quarterback in NCAA history to throw for 2,000 yards and rush for 1,000 in two seasons. Entering his senior season, he is a virtual lock to become the Big Ten's career leading rusher at quarterback. Indiana's Antwaan Randle El has the record with 3,895 yards, and Robinson is second with 3,229.

After his junior season, Robinson looked at potentially leaving Michigan for the NFL but opted to return. Much has been made of his future at the next level, with analysts in agreement that Robinson is a special talent who will play in the NFL—but at slot receiver and in the kick-return game.

The 6'0", 195-pound Robinson has insisted he will play quarterback at the next level.

He has made it this far as a starting quarterback, so why not? Art Taylor, Robinson's coach at Deerfield Beach High, was probably among the first to detect his talent.

"As soon as he stepped on that field his sophomore year playing varsity, we knew we had something special," Taylor said. "I've always said speed kills—there's no substitution for speed. Denard runs a legit 4.3, and that's hard to mess with."

12 Tom Harmon: Heisman Winner

Long before Desmond Howard and Charles Woodson, Tom Harmon was the Michigan player who captivated the nation and won the Heisman Trophy.

Harmon, "Old 98" as he was known, graced the cover of *Time* in 1939, his junior season, and *Life* magazine in 1940, the year he became the Wolverines' first Heisman Trophy winner.

He started that season with a bang, on September 28, his 21st birthday. The Wolverines had taken a historic cross-country flight to Berkeley to face Cal. Michigan's 41–0 victory was the Harmon Show. He took the opening kickoff 94 yards for a touchdown. In the second quarter he returned a punt 72 yards for a score. Let's see, he also had an 86-yard touchdown run, scored on an eight-yard run, and threw for another touchdown in the devastating blowout.

A scout keeping tabs on Michigan for a rival team dominated his notes with thoughts on Harmon from that game. "Whatever you read or hear about Harmon cannot be exaggeration," the scout wrote. "Under no circumstances should the ball be punted to Harmon."

The only loss the Wolverines experienced that season was a 7–6 defeat by Minnesota. Amazingly, Harmon was never part of a team that beat Minnesota, nor did he ever score against the Gophers.

He finished the season in brilliant Harmon fashion at Ohio Stadium. Harmon had a hand in five touchdowns—running for three, throwing for two, and kicking four extra points in a 40–0 win. And when coach Fritz Crisler removed him from the game with 15 seconds left, the Ohio State fans gave Harmon a standing ovation.

Maybe they were just happy to see him go and graduate. Harmon always had played well against the Buckeyes. He missed only three minutes in three OSU games, ran for five touchdowns, threw for four, and kicked seven extra points.

John Sabo in the *Detroit Free Press* wrote, "When Tom Harmon left the field after his third touchdown dash of the day, the whole crowd, friend and foe alike, stood up and cheered. As Harmon left, the Michigan section of the stands emptied. Ten thousand Michigan rooters mobbed Harmon and formed a guard of honor to escort him to the locker room."

Two weeks earlier he had been on the cover of *Life*, with a front-page headline: "Michigan's Great Harmon."

"No. 98 is the most famous football number of the year," it was written in *Life*, referring to the number Harmon had worn since high school in Gary, Indiana. "It belongs to Michigan's great halfback, 21-year-old, 195-lb. Tom Harmon. Every Saturday, while thousands of Michigan alumni and fans scream with excitement, No. 98 runs for touchdowns. His pile-driving legs grind his way through the line. His swivel hips spin him away from tackles. His speed leaves opponents far behind. By mid-season Harmon

Taking It to the Skies

Michigan opened the 1940 season at California, and in those days, train travel was the usual form of transportation for football teams. But this time, the Wolverines would make history as the first college team to make a long-distance plane trip. The school chartered three United Air Lines DC-3s for the two-day, three-stop flight to San Francisco. The planes included a special paint scheme that splashed "Michigan Football Special" across the sides.

There were stops in Des Moines, Denver, and Salt Lake City, where the Wolverines got in an additional practice for the season opener.

Every player under 21 had to have permission from his parents to travel.

fans were so excited they were disappointed if he did not make 70 yd. every time he carried the ball."

Opponents truly couldn't touch Harmon, and he frequently avoided tackles. Even opposing players were awestruck by his ability. During one game, an opponent trying to tackle Harmon got a handful of his jersey number instead (the Wolverines wore tear-away jerseys). After the game, he found Harmon and had him autograph it.

Harmon's "Old 98" jersey was retired when he graduated. In three seasons, he rushed for 2,134 yards, passed for 1,304, and kicked 33 extra points and two field goals. His 33 touchdowns from 1938 through 1940 was then an NCAA record.

Shortly after the Ohio State game, Harmon, who finished second in Heisman voting in 1939 behind Iowa's Nile Kinnick, was awarded college football's biggest prize, the Heisman Trophy.

"I am certain that were it not for Fritz, this halfback would never have gained the honors that came my way during my three years at Michigan," Harmon said years later.

Crisler kept a favorite picture of Harmon standing in the rain on the field at Minnesota, his sleeves ripped off and a large section of his shirt torn out under the right arm. Harmon went through 29 tear-away jerseys his junior year, as would-be tacklers could only grab but not take him down.

"The only thing I ever did for Tom Harmon was make sure he had a football to run with," Crisler said.

After Michigan, Harmon volunteered for the Army Air Corps as an aviator. He was shot down twice and presumed lost, but managed to walk to safety both times. He was awarded the Purple Heart and Silver Star. Harmon later became a sports broadcaster and director. He died in 1990 at the age of 70.

13 Desmond Howard: UM's Second Heisman Winner

He had a 100-watt smile and acrobatic skill.

Diminutive Desmond Howard, who was 5'9" and 176 pounds, was one of the most electrifying players to ever play at Michigan, let alone college football. Howard won the 1991 Heisman Trophy, the second Wolverine to claim college football's biggest prize, and left Michigan with 12 single-season records while having set or tied five NCAA records. The All-American was voted Most Valuable Player by his teammates his senior season, and he also won the Walter Camp Trophy, a player-of-the-year award, and the Maxwell Award.

Clearly, Howard made his mark at Michigan. He is known for "The Catch" against Notre Dame and, more notably, "The Pose," striking the Heisman Trophy pose after scoring against Ohio State in 1991.

Before Michigan, however, Howard was a standout high school tailback at St. Joseph High in Cleveland, where he also led the state in interceptions. When he first arrived at Michigan, the coaching staff thought he would play in the defensive secondary, but a few days into preseason camp, Howard was asked to consider a move to receiver.

"I had to get acclimated to a new position and used to running routes and reading coverages," Howard said. "I think they felt that if they could get the ball in my hands, they had something special."

The Michigan coaches were right, but it took time for Howard to successfully make the position switch. After redshirting his freshman year in 1988, Howard played behind flanker Chris Calloway the following season. The season opener against Notre Dame in 1990 would be his real debut, in a sense. He had six catches for 133 yards and two touchdowns in a loss. He had 140 receiving yards—275 all-purpose—against Michigan State and 167 in the Gator Bowl, in which he had a 63-yard touchdown reception. He was named first-team All–Big Ten, set a school single-season record with 504 yards on kickoff returns, and led the team in catches with 63 and 1,025 yards.

"I gave them an outside weapon," Howard said. "Once we had a legitimate weapon on the outside, I think it complemented our style very well. I just went out there and played ball. Every time I touched the ball, I tried to do something special."

Howard's play was special in 1991. In the second game of the season, with Notre Dame at Michigan Stadium, the Wolverines tried to avoid a fourth straight loss to their rivals. Late in the game on fourth-and-1, quarterback Elvis Grbac found Howard in the back of the end zone, who laid out for the touchdown reception. The play is forever known as "The Catch."

Michigan was 9–1 heading into the regular-season finale against Ohio State at home. Howard returned a punt 93 yards for a touchdown, and when he crossed the goal line, Howard struck the Heisman Trophy pose. The Michigan Stadium crowd—with the exception of Buckeye fans, of course—was delighted. Howard, who has said on multiple occasions that striking the pose was spontaneous and never planned, had 213 all-purpose yards against OSU, including receptions of 50 and 42 yards.

He won the Heisman Trophy by earning 85 percent of first-place votes, at the time the largest margin of victory in the history of the trophy. It should be noted that Michigan never campaigns for individual honors, and the Heisman is no exception.

"I always felt that you should win that award on the field and that your play on the field should speak for itself," Howard said.

In 1991 Howard became the first receiver in Big Ten history to lead the conference in scoring with 90 points. He ranked first nationally in scoring with 11.5 points per game and also led in kickoff returns with an average 27.5 yards. He was tied for second on the NCAA single-season touchdown reception list with 19.

He graduated in the spring of 1992 with a degree in communications and left Michigan with a year of eligibility remaining to enter the 1992 NFL Draft. He was selected fourth overall by the Washington Redskins and became a return specialist in the NFL. Howard, then playing for the Green Bay Packers, was the MVP of Super Bowl XXXI, becoming the sole special-teams player to ever win that award.

14 Charles Woodson: Defensive Greatness

It was plain as day.

He certainly wasn't about to hide his opinion or gloss over it or deny his belief. It was the Monday of Penn State week during the 1997 season, and as Charles Woodson stood at the podium, the very simple question came. He was asked if he was the best player in the country. Woodson did not take long formulating his answer.

"Best player in the country, standing before you," he said without a hint of humor.

Not long after, his self-belief became reality as he became the first primarily defensive player to win the Heisman Trophy. The do-everything junior cornerback also won the Walter Camp Award as college football's best player and the Jim Thorpe Award as the best defensive back. He also was the Big Ten's Defensive Player of the Year for the second straight year and won the Silver Football as the Big Ten's Most Valuable Player. Soon after collecting all that hardware and accolades, Woodson helped lead the Wolverines to a Rose Bowl victory over Washington State and a share of the national championship.

Woodson, raised in nearby Freemont, Ohio, and Ohio's Mr. Football, stood out on a team of special players in 1997. He was praised by his teammates as a leader. On defense, his teammates, especially roommate and starting safety Marcus Ray, often said Woodson covered half the field—he had eight interceptions his junior season and had one apiece in his three final games. As an offensive player, the mere threat of Woodson getting an opportunity to touch the ball scared opponents.

"He can give you nightmares," then–Notre Dame coach Bob Davie said at the time.

He also was a factor on kickoff and punt returns. Quite literally, Woodson did everything. But mostly, he led.

"He led the way, and we followed him," said Michigan tailback Clarence Williams.

Michigan coach Lloyd Carr always knew Woodson was a one-of-a-kind player. After Woodson earned Big Ten Freshman-of-the-Year honors, he suggested to Carr that perhaps he play some receiver. It was an idea Carr already had considered, and he later admitted that he knew it would take time for the Michigan staff to learn how to productively use a two-way player.

Woodson played sparingly on offense as a sophomore, and in the off-season he devoted himself to conditioning. After all, to do all he wanted to do would require him to be in top shape.

"I was ready to do it all," Woodson said of the 1997 season. "I wanted to do whatever I could to help this team win."

He was always a cornerback first, and Woodson truly wanted to strike fear in opposing quarterbacks. He wanted them to be afraid to throw to his side of the field.

The Michigan State game in 1997, a 23–7 Michigan victory, truly was memorable. Quarterback Todd Schultz was intercepted on consecutive MSU possessions in the second half by Woodson.

Charles Woodson celebrates in the second quarter of the 84th Rose Bowl in Pasadena on January 1, 1998.

"They threw the same play at me twice," Woodson said at the time. "I was kind of insulted."

It was especially insulting after the way Woodson made the Spartans pay on the first interception. That one made all the highlight reels. Schultz scrambled toward the sideline and, with no open receivers, he threw toward the sideline. Woodson leaped high in the air, stretched his right arm, and grabbed it with one hand. He later called it the best catch of his life.

It was a stunning display of athleticism, but the Wolverines were not surprised.

"When the quarterback throws the ball, it's like he says, 'It's mine,'" said Andre Weathers, who played cornerback opposite Woodson. "It's almost like he wills the ball to come to him."

A week later against Minnesota, Woodson had one carry, and he scored on a 33-yard run off a reverse.

"If there's a better player in the country, I'd like to see him," then–Minnesota coach Glen Mason said.

The following week in Michigan's statement game against Penn State, Woodson caught one pass and took it 37 yards for a score. Even Penn State's Curtis Enis, a Heisman candidate, was impressed and said, "If I was voting, I'd vote for him."

In his final regular-season game against Ohio State in Michigan Stadium, Woodson had an all-around performance and likely clinched the Heisman Trophy. He had 134 all-purpose yards, caught a pass for 37 yards, returned a punt 78 yards for a touchdown, and recorded three tackles, one pass breakup, and one interception.

Lloyd Carr: Perfect Season, Outstanding Coach

For 13 seasons, beginning in 1995, Lloyd Carr led the Michigan football team as its head coach with his simple and unpretentious manner along with a hard-nosed belief in a strong work ethic and each and every player understanding the value of being Michigan Men.

His legacy is the Wolverines' unbeaten 1997 season that ended with a victory over Washington State in the Rose Bowl—Carr's favorite football venue outside of Michigan Stadium—to clinch a share of the national championship.

Carr went 122–40, and the Wolverines earned at least a share of the Big Ten title five times—1997, 1998, 2000, 2003, and 2004. He spent 28 years at Michigan, which he called at his retirement announcement on November 19, 2007, "the greatest of places."

He was born in Tennessee but moved to Riverview, Michigan, just south of Detroit, when he was 10 years old. Carr played football at Missouri but transferred to and finished his career at Northern Michigan.

His coaching career started at Eastern Michigan, where he was an assistant coach for two seasons, and then he spent two seasons as an assistant at Illinois under Gary Moeller. Moeller and Carr went to Michigan in 1980 to work under Bo Schembechler, where Moeller already had been. Carr worked for Schembechler through 1989, and then Moeller took over as Michigan head coach in 1990. Carr coached the defensive backs the first seven seasons and then became defensive coordinator from 1987 until 1994.

Carr was named Michigan's interim coach on May 13, 1995, in an emotional news conference. Moeller had been involved in a highly publicized incident in a metro-Detroit suburb. Moeller was no longer head coach and Carr, his good friend, was elevated to the interim role.

The 1995 season kicked off with a remarkable comeback victory over Virginia in Michigan Stadium. (The Wolverines had trailed 17–0.) They went 8–2 through the first 10 games of the season, and Carr officially was made head coach on November 13, 1995.

At his retirement announcement, Carr was clear about the head-coaching position at Michigan. He spoke from experience.

"You don't seek this job, the job seeks you," he said.

He remained close to legendary coach Bo Schembechler, Carr's former boss, throughout his coaching career. Schembechler maintained an office in the football building, suitably named Schembechler Hall, and he typically was around during football season. Carr frequently visited with Schembechler, who often gave valued advice.

"[Schembechler] said this to me: 'Look, there's going to be times when you doubt yourself,'" Carr said. "'The reason I know that is that I have doubts about myself. When you have these doubts, just get rid of them because you're prepared and you know what it takes. Go do it.'"

Carr was, in many ways, cut from the same cloth as Schembechler. They were all about integrity and character and demanded that from their players. And as far as the media went, it wasn't that Carr didn't like them, but little leaked out about the team from what they referred to as "Fort Schembechler." He often would spar with the press, offer a lengthy, intimidating stare, and brush off halftime sideline interviews.

Rough edges and all, Carr was Carr, nothing more, nothing less. He was, most of all, a coach whose enjoyment came from teaching, and, of course, winning.

"He does a tremendous job with players," Schembechler once said of Carr. "He knows how to handle players. He's very good at that."

He endured many tests and challenges during his career, and the 1997 season was his highlight. The team reached perfection in terms of its record, boasted a Heisman Trophy winner in Charles Woodson, the Rose Bowl MVP in Brian Griese, earned the AP national championship, and Carr was named National Coach of the Year.

During the 2003 season, Carr entered Michigan history, joining coaching greats Fielding Yost, Bennie Oosterbaan, and Schembechler as the only coaches in the program to coach in 100 or more games. He left the program ranked third in school history in career victories behind his mentor, Schembechler (194), and Yost (165).

Carr's final season in 2007 began with high hopes and a No. 4 preseason ranking, and featured a high-powered roster, particularly on offense. But the Wolverines opened with a shocking loss to Appalachian State that dropped them from the national rankings. Then they were dismantled by Oregon. Injuries to key players took their toll that year, but Michigan managed to win eight straight before losing to Wisconsin and Ohio State.

A day after losing to the Buckeyes, Carr informed his players he would be retiring, confirming yearlong rumors of his departure. He coached one final game, the Capital One Bowl against Florida on New Year's Day. Michigan was unranked, and the Gators were No. 9 and led by quarterback Tim Tebow, who had just won the Heisman Trophy.

Michigan won in stunning fashion, 41–35, and Carr was carried on the shoulders of his players. The Wolverines were No. 18 in the final poll.

"We're going to look back and realize he was special," said former Michigan quarterback John Wangler. "I don't think his greatness will be appreciated until a few years down the road. He was good for the kids. He had everything in perspective."

Carr received one of the biggest honors in college football in 2011 when he was voted into the College Football Hall of Fame.

16 The Story of "The Victors"

Scan different publications and various websites—some with professional contributions, others with opinions from fans across the country—and the bottom line is this: there are those who call it "the greatest fight song ever," as John Philip Sousa reportedly once said, but most—some grudgingly—say it is one of the nation's best and most recognizable fight songs.

Hail, Hail to Michigan

Michigan's fight song, "The Victors," is one of the most recognizable in college football. The song was composed by Michigan student Louis Elbel in 1898 after he watched the Wolverines beat Chicago to win the league championship.

A shortened version of the song, based on the final refrain, is played after the Wolverines score. The full lyrics run more than two minutes long. They are as follows:

Now for a cheer they are here, triumphant!
Here they come with banners flying,
In stalwart step they're nighing,
With shouts of vict'ry crying,
We hurrah, hurrah, we greet you now,
Hail!
Far we their praises sing
For the glory and fame they've bro't us
Loud let the bells them ring
For here they come with banners flying
Far we their praises tell
For the glory and fame they've bro't us
Loud let the bells them ring
For here they come with banners flying
Here they come, Hurrah!
Hail! to the victors valiant
Hail! To the conqu'ring heroes

Hail! Hail! To Michigan
The leaders and the best
Hail! To the victors valiant
Hail! To the conqu'ring heroes
Hail! Hail! To Michigan
The champions of the West!
We cheer them again
We cheer and cheer again
For Michigan, we cheer for Michigan
We cheer with might and main
We cheer, cheer, cheer
With might and main we cheer!
Hail! To the victors valiant
Hail! To the conqu'ring heroes
Hail! Hail! To Michigan,
The champions of the West!

"The Victors," with its military-march feel, is as much a part of a Saturday as is the Michigan football team. When the song is performed, it serves to unite the crowd of Michigan faithful, as they punctuate the "Hail" in the line, "Hail to the Victors," with an upward thrust of their right fist. The song is most prominently on display in a shortened version after the Wolverines score a touchdown or make an interception.

Legendary coach Fielding H. Yost, when once asked about "The Victors," clearly was proud that his high-scoring teams were worthy of such an anthem.

"I reckon it's a good thing Louis Elbel was a Michigan student when he wrote that song," Yost had said. "If he'd been at any other Big Ten school, they wouldn't have had much chance to use it."

Louis Elbel was a junior music student at Michigan in 1898 when the Wolverines headed to Chicago—a team that had beaten Michigan the previous two seasons—with a 9–0 record for the season finale on Thanksgiving Day. Michigan won 12–11 to clinch its first Western Conference title, and Elbel was so elated by the victory, he was moved to create a fight song for the school.

"We were crazed with joy," Elbel later recalled, referring to the Michigan students who had made the train trip to Chicago for the game played in the bitter cold. "We paraded in the dark. We yelled and followed our UM band singing to the tune of 'Hot Time in the Old Town.' It struck me quite suddenly that such an epic should be dignified by something more elevating in music, for this was no ordinary victory.

"My spirits were so uplifted that I was clear off the earth, and that is when 'The Victors' was inspired. I put in a lot of 'Hails,' and I knew the fellows would get them in with the proper emphasis. Through them, the title suggested itself, and I dedicated it to the team of 1898."

Following the game and the parading with his fellow students, Elbel went to his sister's home in Englewood, Illinois, not far from Marshall Field, where the game had been played.

"When I got to my sister's house, somehow I had the presence of mind to write down the notes of that song," he said later. "And when I got to South Bend the next day, I not only tried out the song on my piano, but finished the entire refrain. Then the idea of a big march came to me, and I completed the whole work on the train that took me back to Ann Arbor for Monday's classes."

The song would be published the following year, and in April 1899 John Philip Sousa's band performed "The Victors" for the public in Ann Arbor.

In later years, the song's phrase, "Champions of the West" caused some confusion. It was a reference to Michigan's membership in the Western Conference, which later became the Big Ten. Michigan withdrew from the Western Conference in 1907 and, because that line from "The Victors" was no longer considered fitting, a new fight song, "Varsity," was written in 1911. But the Wolverines returned to the Western Conference in 1917, and "The Victors" said it all.

Former Michigan All-America center Gerald Ford, who later became president, often had the Naval band perform "The Victors" instead of "Hail to the Chief" before state events. Before his death, he had requested "The Victors" be played during his funeral procession.

17 The First Michigan Stadium Night Game

A night college football game is nothing new, but at Michigan Stadium, it was a first on September 10, 2011. Michigan, wearing specially designed under-the-lights "legacy" uniforms, faced Notre Dame, also wearing special uniforms. The rivals ushered in the night-game era at the Big House before 114,804 fans and with the ESPN's *College GameDay* crew on hand.

If the week-long hype wasn't enough, if the night-game setting wasn't enough, Michigan and Notre Dame made things even more memorable on the field in their 39th career meeting. The Irish built a 17-point lead against the Wolverines, who struggled most of the game to find offensive consistency.

But Michigan, led by quarterback Denard Robinson, scored four times in the fourth quarter for a 35–31 comeback victory. It was Roy Roundtree's 16-yard pass reception with two seconds left

Michigan defensive end Will Heininger celebrates with teammates in front of the student section after Michigan defeated Notre Dame, 35–31, in the first night game at Michigan Stadium on September 10, 2011.

that put the exclamation point on the final drive that began on the Wolverines' 20-yard line with 30 seconds remaining.

"I was thinking we were going to win the game, we were going to find a way to get it done," Michigan coach Brady Hoke said of his thoughts with 30 seconds to go.

The Irish totaled 513 yards, but five turnovers tarnished that offensive performance.

Robinson did not have a stellar start to the game and accumulated only 88 total yards in the first half. But he finished with 446 yards, threw for four touchdowns, and rushed for another to overcome three interceptions.

After the game, the Wolverines were enthralled not only by the comeback victory but by what they had experienced in a night-game setting at Michigan Stadium.

"We knew it was going to be crazy, but we didn't know what to expect," Robinson said. "Everyone had maize on, they had had the pom-poms, [and] everybody was like 'Wow, this is a night game at Michigan Stadium against Notre Dame.'"

Hoke has made clear he's old-school and prefers noon kickoffs. But even he enjoyed the spectacle.

"It was a great event," he said. "The enthusiasm, the energy was awesome. Playing it was fun—I had fun."

Safety Jordan Kovacs, a former walk-on from Toledo who had eight tackles and an interception against the Irish, was taken by the stadium at night.

"Michigan Stadium was rocking," Kovacs said. "It was a great game to be a part of. It was fun. I've never seen the stadium like that, and I've been coming here quite a long time."

During the week leading up to the game, Michigan athletic director Dave Brandon said the Michigan–Notre Dame game was the highest-demand ticket in Michigan history. Brandon said another 50,000 tickets could easily have been sold.

Brandon wanted to make certain the first night game went well before he committed to more in the future at Michigan Stadium. Clearly, it was a success, and he said while the goal is one per season, that's no guarantee.

"It would have to be right team, right situation," he said. "I would never commit to every year, but if we could get into that kind of rhythm, that would be terrific."

18 The Game 1973: 10–10 Game, Big Ten Vote

Long after his coaching days had ended, Bo Schembechler would never, ever come close to getting over the way the 1973 season ended.

Schembechler remained bitter until the end.

In the final regular-season game against top-ranked Ohio State, both teams entered undefeated, with the winner knowing it would be headed to the Rose Bowl. Michigan was ranked No. 4.

The Buckeyes led 10–0 at halftime, but Michigan came back and tied the game on quarterback Dennis Franklin's 10-yard run midway through the fourth quarter. Late in the game, the Wolverines were clicking offensively and had moved to midfield. Franklin was hit hard, landed on his right shoulder, and suffered a broken collarbone. With 24 seconds remaining, and a chance to clinch the victory for the Wolverines, Mike Lantry missed on a 44-yard field-goal attempt.

The final score: 10–10 at Michigan Stadium on November 24.

But even after that game had ended, Franklin's injury played an enormous role.

There would be a vote of Big Ten athletics directors to be handled by telephone out of the league's Chicago office, and the outcome would decide whether Michigan or Ohio State would represent the Big Ten in the Rose Bowl. Remember this—the Big Ten had lost four straight Rose Bowls, and as a whole, the athletics directors must have believed the league needed a win in the grand-daddy of them all. Also remember that Ohio State had played in the previous Rose Bowl, and the Big Ten had a no-repeat rule.

Schembechler was in Ann Arbor feeling confident. His team had outplayed Ohio State, and he believed his team was the better of the two. It *had* to be Michigan. Schembechler went about his business and headed to Detroit to tape a television show.

Meanwhile, the athletics directors were individually polled by phone. Michigan's athletics director Don Canham naturally voted for Michigan, and the Wolverines were supported by Indiana, Iowa, Minnesota, and…that's it. Ohio State won the vote 6–4 and would be the Big Ten's representative in the Rose Bowl.

Afterward, the truth started to come out. The athletics directors wondered if Michigan was the representative, would the Wolverines play well enough to win when Schembechler didn't even know the status of his starting quarterback?

"Franklin's injury was the key, I believe," Purdue athletics director George King said at the time.

"I felt the vote should have gone that way [to OSU]," said Cecil Coleman of Illinois. "Franklin's injury was the big factor. If either team had lost its quarterback, I wouldn't vote for that team."

Adding insult to injury, Michigan's in-state rival, Michigan State, cast a vote for Ohio State, courtesy of athletics director Burt Smith. Smith, ironically, was a Michigan graduate.

Schembechler felt robbed, calling the decision a "political thing." Not long before his death in 2006, he reiterated how much that vote stung him and his players.

"[That] was the greatest disappointment of my career," Schembechler said. "We were both undefeated…and we were playing here, and we missed a field goal at the end, and we end up tied. It was a 10–10 tie, and everybody including Woody Hayes congratulated me after the game and said, 'Oh, you'll do a great job in the Rose Bowl,' and all that.

"And everybody expected Michigan to go to the Rose Bowl, because if you look at the game, we outplayed them. If you look at tradition, Ohio State had played in the Rose Bowl the year before, and we used to have a no-repeat rule where you couldn't repeat. So everything indicated that we were going to go to the Rose Bowl."

Many years later, Franklin said in a newspaper story that he was perfectly healthy on January 1, 1974, the day of the Rose Bowl.

"The [Associated Press] sent a reporter to my home in Massillon, Ohio, and took a picture of me throwing a snowball," Franklin said.

19 Michigan Man: What It Means to Those Who Played

No one seems to know exactly when the phrase "Michigan Man" was coined. All anyone seems to know is that legendary coach Bo Schembechler, the quintessential Michigan Man, created it, lived it, and breathed it.

The thing is, everyone who was part of the Michigan program before Bo is considered a Michigan Man. All of those who were part of the Michigan program long after Bo was head coach are also Michigan Men.

But what does it mean to be a Michigan Man?

Who is a Michigan Man?

What are the characteristics of a Michigan Man?

All of that is up to interpretation for those who watch the games, those who coached the games, and those who played the games. Those who attempt to define it say being a Michigan Man means character and integrity; it means dealing with adversity and holding your head high; and it means class and pride.

For those who played at Michigan, it means so many different things on a variety of levels. When the question is posed—"What does it mean to be a Michigan Man?"—they often respond over-whelmed by emotion, choked up by something bigger than they are, but something they assuredly embrace as a means to define themselves as players long afterward.

"It means you uphold what Yost represented and Bo and Crisler and all of those men," said former UM running back Jamie Morris. "You do the things you were taught by the Michigan coaches. You give every ounce of your physical ability in your athletic adventures—I'll call them adventures—and you do the same in the classroom. And you take what you learn here and translate it to your life."

Perhaps the most popular usage of the term "Michigan Man" came in March of 1989 by Schembechler, then the UM athletics director. On the eve of the NCAA tournament, men's basketball coach Bill Frieder agreed to take the head-coaching job at Arizona State, effective at season's end. Schembechler said Frieder's career at Michigan was over. Immediately. "A Michigan Man is going to coach Michigan!" Schembechler proclaimed before promoting assistant coach Steve Fisher.

When Terrance Taylor, a defensive tackle whose last season was 2008, was first being recruited by coach Lloyd Carr, Carr asked Taylor if he wanted to be a Michigan Man.

"I'm like, 'Yeah, sure, I'll be a Michigan Man,'" Taylor said, suggesting that at the time, he was just going along with whatever Carr was pitching. "Now it's like, I'm a Michigan Man no matter what happens. I love Michigan. If you think you're better than me, you're crazy. I know you would die to get a chance to be where I'm at right now.

"Go around and take a poll. A lot of people wanted to come here. It's just understanding. The only way you can understand something that's so big is with time. You talk to a guy like Reggie McKenzie and you understand. Man, he loves Michigan. It almost makes you want to cry."

Morris takes the concept one step further. He believes that fans—men and women—can be Michigan Men and Women.

"You don't have to be an athlete to be a Michigan person," Morris said. "A lot of fans embody what we all do here. They are Michigan people."

20 The Story of the M Club Banner

It is, in many ways, as much a part of the Michigan tradition as are the helmets, the maize-and-blue colors, and Michigan Stadium.

The M Club banner is a 40" x 4' strip of blue material that bears the slogan "Go Blue M Club Supports You," and while the Michigan marching band plays "The Victors," the Wolverines race out of the tunnel and onto the field, where they leap to touch the banner at midfield as they run toward their sideline. It is a pregame tradition carried on before the start of every home game.

"That was a big thing growing up watching Michigan on TV as a little boy," said former UM defensive back and assistant coach Erik Campbell, who watched the Wolverines from his home in Gary, Indiana. "You saw that and you always wanted to touch the banner."

The M Club banner tradition began in 1962 when Bump Elliott was the head coach. The undergraduate M Club started the tradition with a yellow block "M" on a six-foot-wide piece of fabric. Following practice before the Wolverines' 1962 homecoming game against Illinois, the M Club had all of the non-football letterwinners form two lines as the football players ran off the field toward the locker rooms in Yost Field House.

Elliott gave the group permission to recreate that "tunnel" before the game the next day.

A Dastardly Fate!

Traditionally, when Ohio State played at Michigan Stadium, the Buckeyes would run out of the tunnel and break left to their sideline before the game.

But before the 1973 game, John Hicks and the Buckeyes decided tradition would go out the window. Hicks, an offensive tackle, led the Buckeyes out of the tunnel, and they went straight for Michigan's "Go Blue" Banner, held high at midfield for the Wolverines to leap up and touch as they stormed across the field toward their sideline.

Hicks and the Buckeyes tore down the banner and they jumped up and down on it, trying to shred it. The Michigan fans went crazy, and legendary Michigan radio broadcaster Bob Ufer was crazed as he described the scene to listeners—"They're tearing down Michigan's coveted M Club banner!" Ufer shrieked. "They will meet a dastardly fate here for that."

Incensed, the Michigan players stormed the field and jumped and cheered on the sideline before the banner was righted. After a few seconds, the banner was fixed and the Wolverine players ran underneath it. ABC broadcaster Chris Schenkel said, "I don't think I've ever seen two teams more fired up. They can't wait to get after each other."

There is one account that factors in an assist from UM hockey coach Al Renfrew, who won the 1964 national championship, and his wife, Marguerite. Renfrew apparently asked his wife to make two flags to drape over the football locker rooms to cheer on the team.

Marguerite Renfrew, with the help of a neighbor, made the two flags, and the Block M was designed by UM engineering dean Bob Hoisington, to make sure it was accurate (as only an engineer could!). Members of the M Club, of which Renfrew presided over in the 2000–2001 season, then hung the flags in the locker room. They were then moved to the tunnel and then, eventually, the stadium. The flags later morphed into a banner.

Not surprisingly, the banner represents plenty to the players. On special occasions, like the Michigan State game, homecoming, or the Ohio State game, former players line the field and hoist the banner for the current players.

"The banner was an important part of my Michigan experience, because *every* man runs under it and touches it—the All-Americans all the way down to the walk-on guy that gets that All-American ready for the game," said Doug Skene, an offensive lineman in the early 1990s. "The banner is a symbol of Michigan unity. When the banner goes up and it is game time, all of Michigan is together as one, no matter who you are."

Many freshmen have recalled their first time running out of the tunnel to leap and touch the banner. They admit to suddenly doubting their ability to actually reach the banner.

"I remember the first time coming out of the tunnel, you've seen it 1,000 times on TV, but the first time you do it, you have no idea how high it is," Campbell said. "You start to think, *Are you tall enough to reach it?* First you're thinking, *Am I going to fall running out of the tunnel?* and then you worry about missing the banner. You're so nervous as a freshman…I was scared I wasn't going to touch it."

The M Club banner has been stolen twice and was accosted only once by an opposing team—the Ohio State Buckeyes before the 1973 game.

21 1902: Michigan Wins Inaugural Rose Bowl

In the colorful prose of sportswriters in the early 20th century, Fielding Yost's Wolverines were referred to as "Midwest Titans" and they didn't just win, they "vanquished." Such was the case when Yost's "Midwest Titans" went to Pasadena, California, to play in the inaugural Rose Bowl against Stanford on January 1, 1902, the first postseason college football game ever played, beginning the tradition that we now know as the New Year's Day bowl games.

The Tournament of Roses Association had held parades through the pretty Southern California town near Los Angeles for the last decade. The parade was always accompanied by sporting events like tug-of-war and polo, but in 1901, the Association wanted to add football to the schedule and needed to find an opponent for Stanford.

This game was originally called the "Tournament East-West Football Game," with Michigan, obviously, representing the East, and Stanford the West. Yost and his 15 players left Ann Arbor on December 17 and traveled to California via train.

The Rose Bowl stadium was not yet built—it would be ready for the 1923 Rose Bowl game—so the game was played at Tournament Park, about three miles southeast of the current stadium. The park had seats for only 1,000 people, but varying reports indicated that 8,000 to 8,500 fans packed into Tournament Park for the game.

Michigan did "vanquish" Stanford that day 49–0 to clinch the Wolverines' unbeaten season (11–0) and first national championship. Perhaps there was some anger in that score, considering Yost had coached the Stanford team until the school decided that only a Stanford graduate could be its coach.

But while the final score indicated quite a lopsided performance, Stanford gave Michigan a difficult time during the first half. The "Yostmen," as a game summary from that day referred to them, failed on two field-goal attempts from 45 and 25 yards, the latter having been blocked. Late in the first half, Michigan drove to the Stanford 3-yard line but the Wolverines could not penetrate the Stanford defense.

Twenty-five minutes into the game Michigan finally scored, and the Wolverines, as had been the case the whole season, began to wear down their opponent.

"Stanford's men played like demons, but they were sapped from the preparation of the last few days," according to one newspaper game story. "Six of the original Cardinal squad limped to the sideline, and fresh troops replaced them, but Michigan stormed on and redoubled the fury of their attack on Stanford's line."

As the Wolverines continued to pound Stanford, and as darkness fell late in the game, Stanford captain Ralph Fisher approached the Michigan bench and offered to concede the game with eight minutes remaining.

Michigan rushed for 527 yards on 90 attempts—remember, the forward pass was not allowed—and made one of four field-goal attempts. Willie Heston led the Wolverines with 170 yards rushing on 18 carries. Stanford had 67 yards on 24 carries and missed two field goals.

"The 49–0 score speaks for itself," it was written in the game account. "It caps a season that will be long remembered in college football history. Yost's Michigan squad won 11 straight games while outscoring its opponents 550–0."

Perhaps the only downfall was the game prompted Tournament officials to give up football and return to the other sporting events it had hosted. Football returned in 1916, and once the crowds outgrew the available space at the Park, the Rose Bowl was built.

22 The Michigan State Rivalry

Every year during the week of the annual Michigan State game, as if on cue, Michigan players are asked to rank their three rivals—Notre Dame, Michigan State, and Ohio State—in order of importance.

And then they are asked some version of, "So how much do you *really* hate Michigan State?"

In typical, expected form, the answers are always fairly dry and politically correct.

Oh, the Wolverines might talk about their hatred of the color green, since Michigan State's colors are green and white. And those players from the state of Michigan might slyly say they never considered going anywhere to play football except Michigan, but the comments are typically tame and colorless.

Despite being in the same state, the genuine dislike between the Wolverines and Spartans make it a fierce rivalry game every year. Photo courtesy of Per Kjeldsen.

Political correctness aside, this much is true: Michigan players and fans don't like Michigan State players and fans, and vice versa. Well, at least that's the case during rivalry week, which makes it all the more fun. All during that week, stories pepper the local papers and television stations about "mixed football marriages," with one spouse a Michigan graduate, the other a Michigan State graduate. And then there are stories about students at each campus going into protective mode. The Spartan students camp out that week to protect the Sparty Statue from vandalism, just as the Michigan students protect the Block M in the Diag.

This game between two schools separated by about 65 miles is about state bragging rights; it is about the perceived elite nature of Michigan against the agricultural school; and in more recent years, fueled by comments made by former Michigan running back Mike Hart, it is about Michigan playing its "little brother," Michigan State.

Michigan and Michigan State met for the 100th time in 2007. The Wolverines won that game 28–24 at Spartan Stadium, its sixth straight victory in the rivalry. Michigan has dominated the rivalry, but there have been some lean years. Michigan State won four straight beginning in 1934, and from 1950 to 1969, MSU went 14–4–2 before Michigan went on a run of its own: the Wolverines won eight straight and 13 of the next 14.

The cliché about record books being thrown aside is quoted frequently during the week of Michigan–Michigan State. This one is for it all—state bragging rights and the Paul Bunyan Trophy, and frankly that's enough for players from both schools.

Michigan plays Notre Dame in the nonconference part of its schedule, and Ohio State in The Game at the end of the regular season, but Michigan State carries a whole other dimension. Bragging rights are important because so many of the players know each other and see each other throughout the year. It can't feel good for 364 days for the losing players.

Ask those who have played in the rivalry, and they will tell you it's brutally physical.

"I can tell you when I played against those teams, those were the dirtiest players I ever played against in my entire career," Doug Skene, a Michigan offensive guard from 1989 to 1992, said before the 2007 game. "Our senior year, we won 35–10, and I had never been in a game where I had more guys dive at my knees.

"We ran a fourth-and-short in the south end zone—it was a quarterback sneak—and Elvis [Grbac] scored. I was at the bottom of the pile, and I see a green glove coming at me, and the guy is trying to gouge out my left eye. They were taking shots at all of us. I remember in the second half, the refs went to both sidelines, and I remember them telling Coach [Gary] Moeller that this was getting out of hand. We wanted to kill them. We wanted to fight. The Ohio State game is clean, hard, tough football. It's mutual respect. Against Michigan State, I just wanted to break those guys in half. At that time when we played, it was nasty. That is a tough, hard-nosed football game. It's more like a street fight than any other."

Mark Messner grew up in Hartland, Michigan, but went to Michigan where he was a defensive tackle from 1985 to 1988. He lost only once to Michigan State, 17–11 in 1987.

"It's a god-awful thing if you give them those 364 days," Messner said.

To this day, Messner, who lives in Michigan, has come home from a loss to Michigan State and found his home dripping in green-and-white streamers.

Former Michigan quarterback John Wangler (1979–1980) grew up in Royal Oak, a Detroit suburb. He had friends who played for MSU and he absolutely understood why this is such an important rivalry game.

"It's a backyard brawl, it's intense," Wangler said. "The games got a little chippy, no question. If there's anything extra that could be done, it's probably done. The Ohio State game was the ultimate, respectful, all-eyes-of-the-nation-on-you game. This game was more like fighting with your little brother. As far as we're concerned, it was about exerting our dominance in the state."

23 The Notre Dame Rivalry

Michigan–Notre Dame. The Wolverines and the Fighting Irish. You can't separate the two in terms of college football tradition. They are the nation's winningest programs, have the coolest helmets, distinctive uniforms, the unforgettable fight songs, and the great stadiums.

"We're very similar, and that's why the tradition and the battle between the two teams is so rich," former Michigan quarterback John Navarre said. "We have a lot of the same values and traditions."

Michigan has rivalries with Michigan State and Ohio State, but its rivalry with Notre Dame is, well, just different.

"I buy into [the Notre Dame mystique] because there's a mystique about Michigan football," Navarre said. "You've got to have that aura, mystique, that tradition, because the kids who come in there have to believe in that, that there is one there, and once they get there, they buy into it and keep it going. I do believe in it."

Former Michigan coach Lloyd Carr believed, too. "You have the two greatest traditions in college football, and to me, what makes college football special is the tradition—all the great coaches, the great players, the bands, the stadiums, the rivalries that have been created over 100 years," he said. "You can't buy that. It's special because of the tradition. You know it's going to be on national television. Everybody who loves college football will watch or they'll want to watch or they'll be wanting to know what the score is."

The rivalry dates back to 1877, when some Michigan students taught a few Notre Dame students the game. Michigan won the first eight meetings, and after Notre Dame won for the first time in 1909, the series was disbanded.

They resumed the series for two years in 1942 and 1943—the teams split those games, Michigan winning at Notre Dame Stadium in 1942, and Notre Dame returning the favor at Michigan Stadium the next year. It was after that game that Michigan coach Fritz Crisler, despite the urging of Notre Dame coach Frank Leahy to continue the rivalry, said he wanted no more of the series with the Irish.

"There is absolutely no question that a feud of sizable proportion is raging between Leahy and Fritz Crisler," Ed Fitzgerald wrote in *Sport* in November 1943.

Crisler emphasized that conference play was Michigan's focus, and the Michigan–Notre Dame game would take away from the Wolverines' ultimate goal each year of the conference title. Several years later, Bo Schembechler would essentially say the same thing.

"No game can be more important than a conference game, especially Ohio State," Schembechler said. "I always agreed with [Crisler] on that."

In 1946 Crisler backed an official policy that defined the program's schedule process and eliminated Notre Dame from its mix. It was decided that of Michigan's nine regular-season games, only three could be against nonconference opponents. Michigan State was not yet a member of the Big Ten, so the Spartans accounted for one nonconference game, and the other two games would be against a team from the East and one from the West.

Notre Dame was off the schedule.

"I don't know how the rest of the guys felt," Bob Chappuis, a Michigan standout who played for Crisler in 1947 told the *Detroit*

To Hell with Michigan, Notre Dame

Michigan–Notre Dame may be what many call a "natural" rivalry, but there long have been differences and conflicts between the programs.

Notre Dame coach Charlie Weis stirred things up during the spring of 2008 when he spoke to a group of Irish supporters before the spring game in mid-April.

"I've always been one never to make excuses and blow hot air," Weis, speaking into a microphone, said as he walked through the crowd. "Then we'll listen to Michigan have all their excuses as they come running in saying how they have a new coaching staff, and there's changes.

"To hell with Michigan."

Before the teams met that fall, Weis clarified his comments and said it was actually a tip of the hat to former Michigan coach Bo Schembechler.

"Anyone who is a Michigan fan should know and understand that that comment pays respect to Bo and his mentality when playing an opponent," Weis said. "Take it for what it's worth, but I think that's a very respectful comment toward Coach Bo's 'To hell with Notre Dame.'"

Schembechler was never fully in favor of Michigan playing Notre Dame, particularly after the expansion of the Big Ten with the addition of Penn State. He always believed Michigan's focus should be on Big Ten play.

News, "but I was from Ohio—I grew up in Toledo—and all I knew about was Ohio State and Michigan. I just never felt that way about Notre Dame. I didn't like 'em, but I didn't look at them the same. And part of that was due to Fritz Crisler. He said to all of us, a lot of times, 'They call themselves the Fighting Irish, well, they don't have a corner on the word *fight*.'"

The rivalry did not resume until 1978, when Schembechler was head coach. His teams endured a four-loss stretch from 1987 to 1990.

After his coaching days, Schembechler made clear his feelings about playing the Irish.

"We don't need Notre Dame," he said in a 2005 interview. "They need us more than we need them. I would rather have an intersectional game than a Midwest game. Play Southern Cal, I don't care. Play Texas…somebody like that. But not Notre Dame."

Since the series resumed in 1978, Michigan and Notre Dame have met all but six years. In fact, in 2007 the programs agreed to a 20-year contract extension that will have them playing annually through 2031. The series was set to expire after the 2011 season.

"It's a game our players and alumni and every college football fan deserves," Carr said.

24 Bennie Oosterbaan: All-American Athlete

What didn't Bennie Oosterbaan do during his lengthy Michigan career? Oosterbaan, considered one of the greatest all-around players in Big Ten history, was a three-time All-America football player, and he earned nine varsity letters—he was a two-time All-American in basketball and All–Big Ten in baseball. As a senior, Oosterbaan was the football captain, led the Big Ten in scoring during basketball season, and was the Big Ten's leading hitter in baseball.

He later coached at Michigan and won the 1948 national championship, was named Coach of the Year that season, won at least a share of three Big Ten titles, and won the 1951 Rose Bowl.

During his football career, Oosterbaan was a receiver and defensive end, and with quarterback Benny Friedman he was part of Michigan's first great passing combo. As a sophomore in 1925, Oosterbaan led the conference with eight touchdowns, and the Wolverines outscored opponents 227–3. Friedman and Oosterbaan were named All-Americans that season. The two earned that accolade again in 1926, as they helped lead the Wolverines to a 7–1 record. Michigan outscored opponents 191–38, and its only loss was to Navy, a 10–0 defeat on the road.

Oosterbaan still succeeded in 1927 even after Friedman had moved on to the NFL. He was named an All-American for a third time—Michigan's only other three-time All-American came years later when Anthony Carter achieved that status. The Wolverines were 20–4 during Oosterbaan's playing career.

As far as his other collegiate playing careers, Oosterbaan in 1927 became Michigan's first basketball All-American, and also that year, he won the Big Ten batting title. The first baseman/pitcher batted .469.

Oosterbaan coached the Michigan football team for 11 seasons, taking over the team in 1948 when former coach Fritz Crisler named him his successor. Crisler said Oosterbaan had "the best offensive mind in college football." With a team inherited from Crisler, the Wolverines won the 1948 national championship, and they did so with defense. The Wolverines allowed an average of only 70.2 yards rushing.

Oosterbaan Forever an "M" Man

Bennie Oosterbaan, the three-sport standout at Michigan who later would coach the Wolverines, his highlight coming in 1948 with the national championship and coach-of-the-year honors, remains a part of the Michigan campus.

Quite literally.

It was Oosterbaan's wish that after he passed away in 1990, his ashes be placed in the places on campus he felt were dearest to his heart. All-American Ron Kramer, who played for Oosterbaan and loved him dearly, made sure to follow through on his coach's wishes.

Kramer placed some of Oosterbaan's ashes near the stadium tunnel and all around the field. He placed some around Yost Arena, known as Yost Field House when Oosterbaan played basketball there, and also around the baseball field where he also played.

"Ben is everywhere at Michigan," Kramer said.

His teams won Big Ten titles in each of his first three years but did not win another after that. He was 63–33–4 overall during his coaching career.

Oosterbaan was known as a mild-mannered coach who did not rely on yelling and screaming to motivate his players.

"He was a great motivator," Kramer said of Oosterbaan in the *Detroit News*. "He never had much to say, but when he spoke to the players before a game, he spoke in such a sincere way—he was so straight and honest with everyone—that we all believed him. He spoke from the heart, and I can't tell you how many times our teams would go out there and play way over our heads because we loved this man so much."

After Oosterbaan's death in 1990, Kramer scattered his ashes on all the athletic fields where Oosterbaan had starred and earned those nine varsity letters in the mid-1920s. "I told him I would do it," Kramer said. "A little on the football field, the baseball field and track, and a little around the rest of the campus. Ben is everywhere at Michigan."

25 Julius Franks: The First Black All-American at Michigan

Julius Franks was as powerful off the football field as he was on it.

Franks was only the second African American to play for the Wolverines and was the first to earn All-America honors for his play at right guard in 1942. He was a member of the famed "Seven Oak Posts," joining fellow linemen Philip Sharpe, Bill Pritula, Merv Pregulman, Elmer Madar, Robert Kolesar, and Alvin Wistert.

His coach, Fritz Crisler, called Franks one of the hardest-working players he ever coached, but his career was cut short when he and his teammate, Tom Kuzma, contracted tuberculosis. Franks was hospitalized for just more than two years.

It was the end of a Michigan career that started when Franks was voted to the All-City team in Detroit after starring at Hamtramck High in 1939. He was invited to Michigan's annual football bash in Detroit, and that's where he realized his destiny.

"When I saw all the Michigan fellows who were graduating that year stand up and say why it was important to get an education and what it meant to go to Michigan...I decided right then that was the school I wanted to go to," Franks told a reporter.

Franks, who died on November 26, 2008, at the age of 86 in Grand Rapids, was unable to pursue football beyond college, but he returned from illness to graduate from dental school in 1951—he was the lone African American in his graduating class.

He became a civic force in Grand Rapids, working hard to integrate blacks into the community. In 1962, aware that real estate agents would not even show homes in white, middle-class neighborhoods to potential black buyers, Franks and three business partners, Sam Triplett, J.E. Adams, and Joe Lee, purchased 20 acres that were being auctioned by the city.

Their goal was to build a middle-class neighborhood for African Americans, and the news that a group of black investors had purchased land and encouraged black residents to build homes in an area populated by whites caused—expectedly—an uproar.

Franks and his partners, however, remained steadfast.

"We wanted to demonstrate that minority people could not only qualify for housing loans but build and maintain them, too," Franks told the *Grand Rapids Press* in 1992. "The thing the four of us decided was that city government couldn't deny us the right that any other American had."

That parcel of land at the northeast corner of Sweet Street and Fuller Avenue NE became known as Auburn Hills, a community that consists of 51 homes.

Franks never quit, even after contracting Guillain-Barre syndrome, which forced him to retire from dentistry in 1992. He was active in the Urban League, United Way, American Red Cross, Boy Scouts of America, and Rotary Club. He was a member of the Western Michigan University board of trustees. In 2006 the Michigan Alumni Club honored Franks with the Paul. G. Goebel Sr. Distinguished Alumni in Athletics Award.

26 Benny Friedman and the Forward Pass

Benny Friedman has widely been acknowledged as college football's first great passer. Certainly he helped revolutionize the position on the college and professional levels in the late 1920s, moving it from a standard run-only game to a more balanced pass-run offense.

Penn State's loss was Michigan's gain after the Nittany Lions decided Friedman was too small to play college football. Still, as often has been the case throughout the years, Friedman considered transferring his sophomore year because he didn't start the first three games in 1924. He had spent his entire freshman year preparing to play, and he clearly was disappointed he could not display what he had been so diligently developing.

"It was at that time [as a freshman] that I decided what the varsity really needed was a good forward passer, and that if Michigan were to succeed in football, she would have to depend on the forward pass," Friedman said in his 1931 book, *The Passing Game*.

He got his break in 1924 when Fielding Yost, the former Michigan coach, convinced coach George Little to give Friedman the start in the fourth game. He threw a 62-yard touchdown pass and ran 26 yards for a score in a 21–0 victory.

Benny Friedman is shown in this November 1939 photo, warming up for the Cedarhurst (N.Y.) Wolverines, whom he coached and played for. Friedman, one of college and pro football's first great passing quarterbacks, was inducted into the Pro Football Hall of Fame in 2005.

A year later, the man who saw reason to start Friedman—Yost—came out of retirement and reclaimed his job with the Wolverines. Friedman became the full-time starter at quarterback. Joined by sophomore end Bennie Oosterbaan, the Benny-to-Bennie duo became one of the most celebrated pairs in college football. Friedman threw for 11 touchdowns that season, and he handled all the place-kicking. He and Oosterbaan were named All-Americans after they helped the Wolverines outscore their opponents 227–3, win a Big Ten title, and finish ranked No. 2 in the country.

Yost later called that 1925 squad his "greatest team ever." High praise, indeed.

Friedman was even better the following season, his senior year. The Wolverines were 7–1 that season, their only blemish a 10–0 loss to Navy. Friedman helped lead the team to another Big Ten title, not to mention earning All-America honors for a second straight season. And against Ohio State, then the second-to-last game of the regular season, he had a brilliant game. He threw two touchdown passes and kicked the game-winning 43-yard field goal in a 17–16 victory.

The Big Ten named Friedman its Most Valuable Player after that season.

"In Benny Friedman, I have one of the greatest passers and smartest quarterbacks in history," Yost said at the time. "He never makes a mistake, and as for football brains, it's like having a coach on the field when Benny is out there calling signals."

But why was Friedman so important to the college game? Murray Greenberg literally wrote the book on Friedman, *Passing Game: Benny Friedman and the Transformation of Football*. Greenberg described how, because the ball was bigger, fatter, and more rounded, it was hard to grip and throw downfield.

Friedman worked on his wrist and arm strength before, during, and after his Michigan career. He would carry a tennis ball or a handball, constantly gripping and releasing it. He later said that all his exercises helped, and by the end of his freshman year at Michigan, he was able to wrap his hand around the football.

"He had a unique ability to grip the football and throw it down the field with accuracy," Greenberg said in an interview. "Combined with his physical strength, he had nerve. He was completely unintimidated and uninhibited. He'd throw the ball on any down, from anywhere on the field, when that was practically a mortal sin."

Friedman went to the NFL in 1927, and in 1928 he became the first quarterback—and only—to lead the NFL in both rushing and passing for an entire season. He was an All-Pro his first four years.

He is a member of the College Football Hall of Fame, the University of Michigan Hall of Honor, and in 2005 Friedman was inducted posthumously into the Pro Football Hall of Fame. Former San Francisco 49ers coach Bill Walsh honored Friedman at the induction.

"Benny, you were really the catalyst that started the forward pass in professional football," Walsh said. "And, I don't know how long the lack of passing would have gone without your presence, it may have gone on for many years. But you're the person who demonstrated and proved to everyone that the forward pass can be effective and, more importantly, it can be consistently effective."

27 Ron Kramer: Nothing Was Impossible

If Ron Kramer had considered going anyplace else to play college football, well, let's put it this way…there was no other place Ron Kramer was going to play college football.

Kramer was the finest athlete in the state of Michigan, a standout at East Detroit High, from which he graduated in 1953 and where he excelled in multiple sports. But football would be his ticket to Michigan where he would play for coach Bennie Oosterbaan and join incoming freshmen Terry Barr, Tom Maentz, Charlie Brooks, Mike Rotunno, and Jerry Goebel.

"Bennie didn't recruit anybody," Kramer said in an interview long after his Michigan career had ended. "Bennie said if you wanted to go to Michigan, 'It's a privilege.' And if you didn't want to go to Michigan, 'Go someplace else.'"

Kramer didn't go anywhere else, and he certainly went places while with the Wolverines, earning nine varsity letters—he also played basketball and ran track—and All-America status in football.

"To top off his marvelous gifts of size and speed, plus an uncanny coordination, Kramer is one of the fiercest competitors I've ever seen," Oosterbaan had said of Kramer.

The Apple Man

When Ron Kramer was a three-sport star at Michigan—his football jersey No. 87 was retired after his senior season in 1956—there was a man named Mr. Chestnut who would bring two to three bushels of apples to the football facility every Wednesday.

Why Wednesday? Because that was typically the toughest football practice of the week.

Kramer, who played professionally for the Green Bay Packers, decided to carry on that tradition for the current Wolverines.

"A while ago, I decided it was my turn," Kramer said of reviving the apple tradition.

Every Wednesday during the season, Kramer takes three bushels of Michigan-raised apples to the football building now known as Schembechler Hall. The apples await the players outside of the locker room.

In his first season of varsity eligibility in 1954, Michigan won four of its first five games and went on to finish 6–3. Michigan was ranked No. 1 briefly the following season, but a 17–0 loss to Ohio State made news for other reasons. OSU's Hopalong Cassidy fumbled just as he crossed the goal line, and officials ruled it a touchdown. The Wolverines disputed the call, fans threw snowballs, and penalties were handed out. Kramer, however, was ejected.

Kramer maintained for years the ejection was unwarranted, and he had been wronged. Years later, the referee, Tony Skover, reportedly apologized to Kramer at a banquet.

During that 1955 season, Kramer had an incredible performance in a 42–7 victory over Missouri. He caught seven passes—three of which were for touchdowns—kicked five extra points, averaged 41 yards per punt, had two carries, and handled kickoffs.

By 1956, Kramer's senior season, hopes were high for the Wolverines. Kramer and Maentz were featured on the cover of *Sports Illustrated* late in the season, but the Wolverines stumbled in losses to Michigan State and Minnesota to finish 7–2. Amazingly, Kramer never played in a bowl game.

In his senior season, Kramer led Michigan in receptions for the third consecutive season, and he also was used occasionally as a punter, kicker, and running back. He was named an All-American for the second time but finished second in Heisman Trophy voting to Notre Dame's Paul Hornung.

"Nothing was impossible for him," Oosterbaan once said of Kramer. "The impossible was only a challenge."

Kramer was selected in the first round of the 1957 NFL Draft by the Green Bay Packers, where he played for legendary coach Vince Lombardi. He would help the Packers win NFL titles in 1961 and 1962 and played seven seasons in Green Bay, twice being selected an All-Pro tight end. Kramer's pro career ended in 1967 after three seasons with the Lions.

His jersey No. 87 is one of five retired by Michigan. Kramer is a member of the College Football Hall of Fame, National Football Foundation Hall of Fame, and the Michigan Sports Hall of Fame.

28 Tailgating, Michigan Stadium—Style

A trip to Michigan Stadium to catch a football game would hardly be complete without the tailgating experience. Tailgates are sprinkled around the stadium in a number of different parking lots and at nearby homes along the crowded roads that lead to Michigan Stadium. They are hosted at motor homes or under tents with tablecloths and candelabras. Some are extremely low-key—an open car trunk and sandwiches and drinks made available from within—while others are housed inside the garage or on the front porch of a nearby Ann Arbor home.

The bottom line is the experience.

Tailgates are about gathering before a game, eating and socializing, and, if all goes well, there's a postgame tailgate to celebrate a victory while letting the traffic die down.

"There are so many different ends of the spectrum," said Michigan alum Matt Riley, who hosts a game-day tailgate. "It's interesting to see it all."

Riley's tailgate is located across from Michigan Stadium at a home he rents to students, but he has worked into the contract that home-game Saturdays are all about the party. A maize-and-blue sign hanging from the gutter out back carries the name of the tailgate: "The Wolverine Little House." Typically, he and his cohosts will have about 150 guests, but if it's a big game—Michigan State or Ohio State—the crowd nearly doubles. Over the years it became such a popular tailgate, they started to make a guest list.

"Once you're on the list, you're always on the list," Riley said, laughing.

It is a day-long party at the Wolverine Little House. If it's a noon game, for instance, a full breakfast is served three hours earlier. After games, the grill is hot and there are burgers, brats, and chicken breasts made available. For the bigger games, particularly those with a 3:30 PM kickoff, the menu usually includes a pig roast and about 80 pounds of chicken. For the Michigan State game in 2008, 257 attended, and there was a 150-pound pig roasted and 10 25-pound stuffed turkeys.

"When you think about the number of hours you put into that day, it's just so fun," Riley said. "The tailgates are a blast."

Theresa Wangler is a delightful woman who continues to run a tailgate even though her son, former Michigan quarterback John Wangler, has been out of football for several years. In fact, when Wangler played for the Wolverines, his mother's version of a tailgate was cooking a bunch of food and then taking it to his apartment.

She eventually started tailgating outside Michigan Stadium, and things started small—sandwiches, drinks, and desserts.

"Then it grew and grew and grew," she said. "Now we're feeding anywhere from 50 to 150 a game."

Wangler tries to keep the menu unique and interesting, but the last home game always features chili, and there's always a big bowl of candy. Her canopied tailgate now boasts a sign made by a friend: "Mrs. Wangler's Tailgate Café." Because her son played football at Michigan and remains active in the community, many former players drop by the café for the pregame tailgate.

"It's one big family," she said. "Everyone is very, very friendly. It is a party, but it's a lot of work, and people say to me, 'Why do you do this? It's so much work.' But it's eight games, and all day Friday I cook, and really, 16 days out of the year is nothing. It's a nice thing to do."

How nice?

"We even serve the enemy," Wangler said, laughing. "Ohio State people often stop by and ask, 'Is this where you get free chili?' And I always tell them, 'Yes, this is the place.' We are very nice to our enemies."

One of the most well-known Michigan tailgates, and probably the largest, had to be folded during the 2008 season because of the Michigan Stadium renovation. Ira Jaffe's tailgate, which had been running full-force for 10 years, hosted up to 2,000 fans per home game and was open to anyone.

Jaffe said he was inspired to start his tailgate because of his childhood memories of attending Michigan home games with his father. They would park near the stadium, eat the sandwiches they brought, and then head to the game.

"It's one of my things, yes, to entertain before a game," Jaffe said. "It's also my personality to say, 'Stop by for a drink, stop by for a sandwich,' so it grew and grew and grew. It is [expensive], but it felt good to do it."

Jaffe's memorable tailgate was located on a hill within the Victors Club parking lot. He would carpet the hill, bring in chairs, about 20 tables, plates, napkins and cups, generators if they were going to serve ice cream, 600 bagels, 20 dozen doughnuts, and assorted foods. He and his cohorts drove a Ryder truck and a motor home, and, even with nearly a dozen people helping, it often took close to four hours to wash everything and prepare for the next tailgate.

"When you lose the game, it's sometimes harder to clean up," Jaffe said.

There's absolutely no doubt a Michigan football Saturday would be incomplete without the experience of a tailgate, whether a more structured setting like the Wolverine Little House or Mrs. Wangler's Tailgate Café or something much less organized, like a couple fans using a portable grill outside their car.

It's a must.

"We try to have a good time and make it fun for everyone else," Riley said.

29 What to Do on Game Day in Ann Arbor

Tailgating before a Michigan football game might be enough for most fans, but it isn't all you can do on a Saturday, whether it's an early noon start or kickoff is later on. Ann Arbor is a terrific city, with an active downtown area featuring shopping and restaurants, and the campus area, of course, is filled with eateries, bookstores, and shops offering a local flair.

If you arrive early enough on a game day or even the day before, and there's time to spare, get into the spirit by driving around the Michigan athletic "campus." The football building, which houses all of the coaches' offices, team meeting rooms, the athletic training room, and locker room, is appropriately called Schembechler Hall. Next door is Oosterbaan Fieldhouse, which has been the location of the football team's indoor facility. A new indoor structure to replace the outdated fieldhouse will soon be unveiled adjacent to Schembechler Hall.

Not far from there is Yost Ice Arena, a grand brick facility that is worth stopping by to check out. There is plenty of hockey memorabilia, and if there happens to be a hockey game the same weekend as football, definitely make that a destination—few arenas can duplicate the atmosphere of Yost. Also nearby is Revelli Hall, where the band practices. If it's a nice day, you just might be lucky enough to witness practice.

One must-see area on campus is the Diag. It is a large, open area in the middle of the central campus, and its name comes from the many sidewalks that run through or near it in diagonal directions. It is one of the busiest areas on campus. A brass Block M is embedded at the center of the Diag, and during the week of the annual in-state rivalry football game against Michigan State, members of the Theta Xi fraternity take turns guarding the M to prevent Spartan fans from vandalizing it.

There are plenty of restaurants around town that will give you a local feel for Ann Arbor. For breakfast before a game, try Angelo's on Catherine Street and sample the raisin bread french toast. A terrific spot for lunch is Zingerman's on Detroit Street, founded in 1982 and considered among the nation's top delis.

Other restaurant stops to consider are Dominick's, located on Monroe Street and open from March to November. It is noted for its sangria and outdoor seating and atmosphere, so an early season game weekend would be best. Cottage Inn Pizza typically is packed after a football game—you'll often find players and their families dining there. The Brown Jug, another favorite, features menu items that carry the names of current coaches and former players, such as the "Jamie Morris Salad" and "Leach's Chicken Picatta Pasta."

The restaurant, which contains plenty of Michigan football memorabilia, is located on University Avenue.

Several former Michigan players recommend Pizza Bob's on State Street. One of the menu items worth trying is the "chipati," a salad stuffed into a pocket of bread and topped with a secret sauce.

Of course, the game-day experience wouldn't be complete without wearing the appropriate maize-and-blue apparel. Among the top shopping choices for all things Michigan are the M Den, which has a location on State Street and also outside the stadium, and Moe Sports Shop on University.

30 Gerald Ford: UM's Own

Long before Gerald Ford became the nation's 38th president, he was a standout All-America center on the Michigan football team.

Ford, from Grand Rapids, played on the 1932 and 1933 national championship teams and was voted the Wolverines' Most Valuable Player his senior year in 1934. He played in the annual East-West Shrine Game in San Francisco on New Year's Day in 1935.

After graduating from Michigan in 1935 with a degree in economics and political science, Ford received contract offers from the Detroit Lions and Green Bay Packers, but he instead attended law school at Yale. He helped put himself through school by working as an assistant football coach and freshman boxing coach.

Michigan retired Ford's No. 48 jersey at halftime of Michigan's game against Michigan State on October 8, 1994. It is one of only five numbers that have been retired in the history of the program.

"Other honors that have been bestowed on me were because of my work or my efforts," Ford said at the time of his jersey-number

Gerald Ford won three varsity letters as a lineman and was voted Most Valuable Player in 1934 playing center for Michigan. He later took part in the Shrine Bowl and Pro-All Stars games. At Yale University Law School, he served as assistant varsity football coach to Ducky Pond and was freshman boxing coach.

retirement. "But in this case I am being honored by a school where I learned skills and discipline that I used for the rest of my life."

Ford was 93—the longest-living president—when he died on December 26, 2006, at his home in Rancho Mirage, California. At the time, the Wolverines were about 130 miles west in Los Angeles preparing for a Rose Bowl game against USC. Then–Michigan coach Lloyd Carr, who had several interactions with Ford, spoke to his players during a team meeting the day after Ford's death and shared with them some of the many stories he had.

"[Ford] always told the players when he talked to them—and here's a man who for a period of time was the most powerful man in the world, he played football [at Michigan] in the mid-'30s, in the middle of the Depression, he cleaned dishes at the [Michigan] Union—and he always reminded them they were the luckiest guys in the world because they got to play football," Carr said.

Ford nearly quit the team in 1934 because of controversy involving his African American teammate Willis Ward, with whom Ford roomed on the road. Michigan was to play Georgia Tech that fall, but Georgia Tech was not going to play if Ward participated. Ward, who earned a law degree and became a lawyer and judge, did not play, and he later recalled in an interview that Ford had considered quitting the team in protest.

In a 1999 op-ed piece in the *New York Times*, Ford defended Michigan's affirmative-action admissions policy and referenced his former teammate. "Do we really want to risk turning back the clock to an era when the Willis Wards were isolated and penalized for the color of their skin, their economic standing, or national ancestry?" he asked.

Michigan football was never far from Ford's heart or interest. He attended practices and games when possible. He spoke to the team

Celebrity Guest List

Michigan isn't just a football school, you know. In case you don't believe it, take a look at the celebrated alums who had nothing to do with football or athletics while attending school in Ann Arbor.

Among the more famous: actor James Earl Jones, comedienne Gilda Radner, actor David Allen Grier, actress Lucy Liu, playwright Arthur Miller, and journalist Mike Wallace.

The three-man Apollo 15 crew that flew to the moon from July 26 through August 7, 1971, was an all-Michigan group. They were Col. David Scott, Maj. Alfred Worden, and Col. James Irwin. It was the first expedition with a lunar rover vehicle, used by Scott and Irwin on the surface of the moon. They carried with them three Michigan-related items—a miniature UM flag, a seal from the department of aerospace engineering, and a charter of the UM Alumni Club of the Moon, which was left on the surface.

in 1976 before a team meal at the student union and, as always, reminded them how much a degree helped long after football.

"Coming to the campus brings back some great memories," Ford told the team. "I can recall vividly my freshman year. We couldn't play on the varsity in the freshman year. And I ate a few meals here in the Union, and I really got to love and feel very strongly about this university. I think it has contributed very significantly to whatever success I've had.

"The friends I made and the opportunities educationally and the whole atmosphere here was a great factor in the incentive and the drive to do as well as one could. I am very proud of the great record that you have and the way you play football. You play to win, and that's the only way I know to move ahead."

Legendary coach Bo Schembechler gave an interview in August 2006 describing how Ford often visited the team.

"At practice he would say, 'Bo, do you mind if I get in the huddle?'" Schembechler said. "There was one rough-looking Secret Service guy that always was looking over President Ford's shoulder. Once when the president was leaning into the huddle, the Secret Service guy was standing between the ball and the huddle, and our quarterback said, 'What should I do?' And I said, 'Run over him.'"

31 Brian Griese: Walk-On QB Makes Good

Imagine if Brian Griese had decided to leave Michigan after his fourth season in 1996, taken his Michigan degree, and moved on into the business world. That is exactly the scenario Griese was considering even after the successful completion of his senior season. In Michigan's regular-season finale at Ohio State in 1996, Griese got his chance when, just before halftime, starting quarterback Scott Dreisbach left with a mild concussion and injury to his right elbow.

Michigan trailed 9–0. But on the second snap of the third quarter, Griese hit Tai Streets on a 69-yard touchdown pass that sparked a 13–9 upset of the Buckeyes.

"That's why you play the game," Griese said. "You never know what's going to happen on the next snap. A whole season, or a whole career, can change."

He earned the start in the Outback Bowl, and played well in a 17–14 loss to Alabama, but the former walk-on remained conflicted about his future. During that bowl trip in Tampa, Griese dined one night with his older brother, Jeff, and his father, Bob, who knows a thing or two about quarterbacking. Something his father said that night stuck.

"When he came [to Michigan], he said he wanted to help get them to the Rose Bowl," Bob Griese said. "I said, 'You'd feel awfully bad if they went to the Rose Bowl this year and you weren't around.'"

Done deal.

Griese stuck around for his fifth season and the rest, as they say, is history. He led Michigan to its first perfect regular season since 1971, its first Rose Bowl in five years, and most important, its first national championship since 1948.

Griese said he knew after Michigan defeated Colorado 27–3 in the 1997 season opener that he had made the right decision to stay. That season was a stellar ending to a sometimes difficult career.

When Dreisbach, then a redshirt freshman, suffered a season-ending thumb injury early in the 1995 season after going 4–0 as a starter, Griese entered and went 5–4 as the starter. The following spring, Dreisbach was back, reclaimed his job, and Griese got involved in an incident at a local bar. He was suspended from the team and worked out on his own.

By the fall, Dreisbach had the job sealed for 1996, and Griese rode the bench. He was a holder on field goals and extra points, and he was called upon to pooch-punt. Still, though unhappy, he maintained his poise and continued to prepare as though the starting job was his. And then came the injury in the Ohio State game, and Griese was back on the field.

"He never lost faith in himself, and we all do," said Stan Parrish, then Michigan's quarterbacks coach. "When things don't go well, you doubt yourself, you get down in the dumps. It's easy to give in and easy to give up. He's got a little something inside that kept him going."

Griese earned the starting job in 1997. Described as "businesslike" by his teammates, Griese threw for 2,293 yards, completed 63 percent of his attempts, and had 17 touchdowns with just six interceptions to help lead the Wolverines to a perfect season. That snapped Michigan's string of four straight four-loss seasons, and Griese, who was 17–5 as the starter, quarterbacked three straight victories over Ohio State.

Michigan coach Lloyd Carr frequently referred to him as "the most underrated quarterback in the country"—Tennessee's Peyton Manning and Washington State's Ryan Leaf garnered all the attention at the time. Griese was MVP of the Rose Bowl, passing for 251 yards and three touchdowns, including passes of 53 and 58 yards to Streets in the victory that clinched a share of the national championship.

"It's something special, and I'm happy that when I'm older in life, I can tell my kids that we won the championship at Michigan in my last year after going four years of not being able to do it," Griese said. "I can tell them about being persistent and not giving in and saying, 'Well, I might not play so I'm not going to come back.'"

32 The Wistert Brothers: A Hall of Fame Family

The Wistert Brothers—Francis, Albert, and Alvin—each wore No. 11 during their storied Michigan football careers, each played tackle, all three were first-team All-Americans, and all three have been inducted into the College Football Hall of Fame and into the Michigan Hall of Honor. Their shared jersey number is one of five that has been retired by the Michigan football program.

"If I'm not mistaken, I think this is unprecedented in the annals of college football that three brothers all would go to the same school, all played football, all played tackle, all wore the same No. 11, all made All-American," Alvin Wistert said in an interview with the *Detroit News*. "Two of us played on four national championship teams, and all were inducted into the College Football Hall of Fame."

Francis "Whitey" Wistert was the first of the brothers to play for Michigan. He played on the 1931, 1932, and 1933 teams, all of which won Big Ten titles, and the '32 and '33 teams were voted national champions. He was also the Big Ten's Most Valuable Player in baseball in 1934 and played professionally for the Cincinnati Reds.

Whitey Wistert was attending high school in Chicago when his friend, John Kowalik, who happened to play football, was invited to visit Michigan and take a friend. Whitey and Kowalik went for the visit together.

"And that's how it started, the Wisterts of Michigan," Alvin said in the interview.

Albert "Ox" Wistert was four years younger than Alvin, but he was the second of the brothers to play for the Wolverines. He played with Tom Harmon, Michigan's first Heisman Trophy winner, in 1940, and also played in 1941 and 1942, when he was named the Wolverines' Most Valuable Player. He was the only Wistert to play professional football. He played nine years for the Philadelphia Eagles and was a four-time All-Pro.

Alvin "Moose" Wistert was the last of the three to play at Michigan, and he had the most interesting journey to Ann Arbor. Moose, who didn't play sports in high school, was a salesman until World War II and then served four years in the U.S. Marine Corps. After spending a year at Boston University, he enrolled at Michigan in 1947 at the age of 31, becoming the oldest man to play football for the Wolverines and one of the oldest to play college football. He was part of the national championship teams in 1947, earning a spot on defense as a sophomore that season, and in 1948. He finished his college career after the 1949 season.

So much has been written about Fritz Crisler's 1947 team and its offense, the "Mad Magicians," but Alvin Wistert said that team was strong defensively, as well.

"[Crisler] would get the scouting report, and Fritz would go over it, telling us, 'Before they go across midfield, they're apt to do so and so,'" Wistert said in another interview. "The offensive plays would unfold just as he said they would. It was amazing. I would think, *My God, they're doing what he said they would.*"

33 The Captains Tradition

Run down the list, and it looks like a "Who's Who" of Michigan football. Dave DeTar was the first in 1879, and his name is atop an impressive number of men who went on to become captains in the Michigan program. In 1927 Bennie Oosterbaan was captain, Forest

Evashevski held the position in 1940, Ron Johnson in 1968, Rob Lytle in 1976, Mark Messner in 1988, Jarrett Irons in 1996, and LaMarr Woodley in 2006, just to name a few.

Until 1970, Michigan had single captains. From that year on, two or more players were voted captains before each season by their peers.

"I learned this from Jimmy Harbaugh, that regardless of what you do, what you want, it's about getting your team to play its best," Corwin Brown, a captain in 1992, said of Harbaugh, a captain in 1986. "When they need you most, you have to be at your best—you don't have to be at your best physically, but you have to do whatever you have to do to get your team going."

Former Michigan coach Lloyd Carr said the responsibility is like no other.

"The greatest honor a Michigan football player can receive is to be selected by his teammates as captain," he said.

Quarterback John Navarre was voted a captain in 2003, along with defensive teammates Grant Bowman and Carl Diggs. Navarre said you learn about how to be a captain from those that came before and led by example, or vocally, or both.

"There is great communication from all the captains," Navarre said. "They have great leadership. They're approachable and they reach out to the younger guys because they realize that we need everybody in this program in order to win a championship. Communication, leadership, and being a consistent performer on the field are all key characteristics that our captains have had."

Bowman echoed Carr in saying that being elected a captain by your peers is the biggest vote of confidence a player can receive. "It [was] an honor for it to come from a team I respect so much," Bowman said.

Brown, a safety, was a boisterous, verbal leader who also led by example. He still remembers the moment he found out he had been elected. "I was humbled," Brown said. "I didn't feel any pressure because I knew what to do and I knew what it took. It's hard

O Captain! My Captain!

The Michigan football team has been represented by at least one captain since the very beginning, when Dave DeTar held that role in 1879.

When Bo Schembechler arrived at Michigan in 1969, he made one change that became effective the following year that allowed the players to vote for cocaptains. The last individual captain at Michigan was tight end Jim Mandich in 1969.

There have been two brother tandems to serve as captains at Michigan. Pat and Mike Massey were captains their senior seasons. Pat was a cocaptain in 2005 and Mike in 2008. Mike and Doug Mallory also were captains. Mike was a two-time captain in 1984 and 1985, and Doug was elected in 1987.

For the first time in program history, three defensive linemen were elected captains in 2008—Tim Jamison, Will Johnson, and Terrance Taylor.

Mike Mallory wasn't the only player to be elected captain more than once during his playing career. The others were Jake Long (2006, 2007), Steve Hutchinson (1999, 2000), Jon Jansen (1997, 1998), Jarrett Irons (1995, 1996), Robert Thompson (1981, 1982), Kirk Lewis (1975, 1976), Angus Goetz (1919, 1920), George Dygert (1892, 1893), John Duffy (1887, 1888), and Horace Prettyman (1884, 1885, 1886).

to explain, but I felt great. When you take on the role as captain, there's so much behind you, you can't lose or fail. It actually empowers you. Whatever good qualities you have in you, if you embrace it, it makes you a better person, a better leader. That's what Michigan is all about."

The key for any captain, Navarre said, was to not change the way he behaves in certain situations or how he reacts. He is elected for a reason, after all.

"Because of the way you are and the way you carry yourself in the off-season building up to [the season]," he said. "You don't want to go changing who you are because you were elected captain. You don't want to change the way you act just because you've been selected as a captain. You don't have to do anything extra because you're a captain, since you've been named captain for a reason."

Coach Rich Rodriguez in 2008, his first season with the Wolverines, altered the traditional election of captains for the first time in the 129-year history of the program. Captains were not elected before the season. Instead, Rodriguez and his staff each week named four "game captains" who walked to midfield together for the pregame coin toss. The week before the final regular-season game, captains were elected by their teammates.

For the first time in the history of the Michigan football program, four captains were elected in 2008—fifth-year seniors Mike Massey, a tight end, and defensive linemen Tim Jamison, Will Johnson, and Terrance Taylor.

What do all Michigan captains that have spanned generations have in common?

"We're all the same," Brown said.

34 The Little Brown Jug

The Little Brown Jug looks like, well, a smallish, old-fashioned, earthenware, five-gallon brown jug. But in Michigan lore, it is so much more.

Ask any Wolverines who have enjoyed hoisting the Jug after a victory over Minnesota, and the reality is evident—keeping the Little Brown Jug in Schembechler Hall is absolutely mandatory.

First, though, a history lesson. In 1903 Michigan coach Fielding Yost took his Wolverines to Minneapolis to play the Golden Gophers, which was a very strong team that season and 10–0 with Michigan coming to town. Before the game, Yost, not trusting his hosts to give him and his team clean water—also fearing some rabid Minnesota fans might taint the water—sent team manager Tommy

Coach Bump Elliott proudly displays the Little Brown Jug on October 26, 1968, after Michigan's 33–20 win over Minnesota.

Roberts to purchase some kind of drinking receptacle from a store in Minneapolis. Roberts bought the jug for 30¢.

The Wolverines took a 6–0 lead early in the game, but with less than two minutes to play, the Golden Gophers scored to tie the game. Fans stormed the field, and when they refused to return to their seats, the game was called with time remaining on the clock.

Eager to get out of town quickly, Yost and the Wolverines rushed to the team bus. The jug was left behind in the University of Minnesota Armory.

Minnesota equipment manager Oscar Munson found the jug the next morning and took it to athletics director L.J. Cooke, saying simply, "Yost left the jug." Minnesota then painted the putty-colored jug brown, added the score from that 1903 game, and inscribed it: "Michigan Jug, Captured by Oscar, October 31, 1903."

Yost, realizing the jug had been left behind, wrote Cooke and requested the jug's safe return. Cooke replied, "If you want it, you'll have to come up and win it."

A Trophy to Behold

The oldest trophy game of which Michigan is a part is against Minnesota for the Little Brown Jug. On the line in the Michigan–Michigan State rivalry since 1953, the year MSU joined the Big Ten, has been the Paul Bunyan Trophy.

It is a rather large four-foot carved wooden statue of Paul Bunyan astride an axe with his feet planted on a map of the state of Michigan. Two flags, one feature the Michigan "M" and the other with the Michigan State "S", are on either side of Bunyan, and he sits atop a five-foot stand.

About a month before Michigan and Michigan State played each other in 1953, the state's governor, G. Mennen Williams, proposed that the teams play for the Governor's Trophy to honor that first game as Big Ten opponents. Williams commissioned a Chicago jeweler for $1,400 to carve the trophy from wood.

Michigan was not thrilled about this new trophy. The Wolverines already played for the Little Brown Jug, and they did not want its importance diminished by this giant wooden Paul Bunyan Trophy.

Michigan State won the first Bunyan Trophy game 14–6 in East Lansing. The following season, Michigan won 33–7 at Michigan Stadium, but the trophy was left on the field for about a half-hour—the Wolverines did not realize they had to keep the trophy. They did claim it, but did not engrave their winning score; Michigan State did it for them in 1956 after reclaiming the trophy with a 9–0 victory.

Early in 1955, the Paul Bunyan Trophy went missing from Michigan. It later was discovered that Michigan students had taken it as a prank.

In 1958 the teams tied 12–12 in Spartan Stadium. Michigan, according to the student newspaper, refused to take it. The Spartans had been heavily favored entering the game and were embarrassed by the tie—they didn't want the trophy, either, but eventually took it.

Because of the craziness of that 1903 game, the teams did not play again until 1909 in Minneapolis. Michigan returned to Ann Arbor with the Jug after a 15–6 victory.

That Little Brown Jug has been well-traveled. It disappeared from the trophy case at Michigan in 1930 and was not found until 1934 when an Ann Arbor gas station attendant found it behind some bushes. While the original jug was missing, a replica was placed in the Michigan trophy case.

Michigan has dominated the rivalry with Minnesota and has enjoyed the Jug, which now is painted half blue and half brown and features the scores from every game. The longest stretch the Golden Gophers have possessed the trophy was nine years beginning in 1934. They also had it for a four-year stretch beginning in 1960.

During Lloyd Carr's tenure as Michigan head coach, on the Monday of Minnesota week each year, he would open his remarks to the media with the history of the Little Brown Jug, telling the story in great detail.

"It has a great tradition and a great meaning here," Carr said. "When you lose it, it's a miserable experience. When you win it, you get to keep that jug where it belongs.

"I mean, we bought that jug."

35 The Tradition of the Michigan Stadium Tunnel

It is dark and somewhat cavernous, often damp with sweat and water, and it is here that both football teams gather on game day to make their journey to the Michigan Stadium field.

Michigan players exit their locker room and turn left to head down the tunnel. Above them, as they start to make their trip toward the field, a short wall drops from the ceiling, and it is painted blue with maize letters that read: Go Blue.

This is where the Wolverines gather themselves as individuals but unite as a team. Some are in a zone and focused in, others are full of energy and bouncing, others are talking and clapping, getting even more motivated for the game that's about to begin.

It feels like a long walk, but it doesn't take much time to reach the entrance to the field. There is a subtle grade change as the tunnel nears its opening. To either side, the seating is exposed, and fans can lean toward the players to slap their hands or yell encouragement. (If you're an opposing player, encouraging words are probably *not* what you're hearing.)

"That tunnel should be marked as a historical site," said former Michigan offensive lineman Doug Skene. "The list of men that have walked that tunnel is impressive."

When asked one day what it is a Michigan fan should do to really live the Michigan experience before he or she dies, former running back Jamie Morris replied quickly and jovially, "Run down the tunnel onto the field!"

While there is security before and after games at either end of the Michigan Stadium tunnel, fans have been known to trickle in. There have been opportunities for fans to experience the tunnel and imagine themselves as Michigan football players making their way to and from the locker room.

Included in both "fantasy camp" experiences for Michigan male and female fans is a run through the tunnel. Fan days that have been held in Michigan Stadium to introduce the upcoming team allow fans access to the tunnel, and the annual Big House Big Heart 5K Run is another way to get a first-hand look, while also raising money for charity. The run begins outside the stadium and ends with participants running through the tunnel, onto the field, and finishing at the 50-yard line. They also can see themselves on the scoreboard as they finish the run.

And while the tunnel is a very cool experience for fans, imagine what it's like for the players. Each time they go through the tunnel feels different.

"I had been down that tunnel many times before when the stadium was empty for practices, conditioning, or pictures," Skene said. "However, the first game day was marked on my mental calendar from the moment I shook Bo's hand and committed to UM.

"When you have earned the uniform and walk the tunnel, you know that you are one of about 115 men on the face of the earth that is lucky enough to look out across the field to the packed seats, the 'Go Blue' banner dead ahead, and the band ready to blast 'The Victors' at the drop of the conductor's wand."

While the experience itself may have been the same home game after home game, running through the tunnel for the players never grows old.

"It was awesome the first time, it was awesome every time, and it was even awesome the last time," Skene said. "Many nonplayers walk that tunnel on game day. Police, administrators, media, some fans, and even former players are in there every game day. However, it is not the same as when you have the uniform on, and you are about to take the field and fight for Michigan!"

36 Jake Long: Taken No. 1 in 2008 NFL Draft

Long before Jake Long became the first overall pick in the 2008 NFL Draft, and long before Jake Long became the highest-paid lineman in the NFL, he was Jake Long, the soft-spoken, enormously talented kid from East Lapeer High in Michigan.

He had grown up a Michigan fan and wanted to play football wearing the famed winged helmet, so when then–Michigan coach Lloyd Carr drove to Lapeer for a recruiting visit to meet the person who would go on to become one of the program's greatest linemen, he was first greeted by the high school band.

Carr was charmed by the moment. He was more overwhelmed by the talent on his hands, later saying Long played in a "different dimension."

The 6'7", 315-pound Long started 40 games at Michigan, was the Big Ten Offensive Lineman of the Year in 2006 and 2007, finished second to LSU defensive tackle Glenn Dorsey in voting for the Lombardi Award and Outland Trophy, and, perhaps most important, he was voted the Wolverines' captain his junior and senior years.

Those who played with and coached him said he was as nice a guy away from football as he was ferocious during games.

"I'm mean on the field," Long said. "I'm a very nice guy off the field. When I buckle up that helmet, I change. It's football mode. I go out there and try to bury the guy and make sure they don't touch the quarterback or running back."

Long was a certain first-round NFL pick after his junior season, but with unfinished business with the Wolverines, he chose to return for his final year of eligibility. When Long decided to fulfill his senior season with the Wolverines, eventual all-time leading rusher Mike Hart followed suit.

"If Jake was leaving, I was leaving, definitely," Hart said shortly before the 2007 season. That's how much Long meant to the Michigan offense.

He gave up only three sacks in his final 26 games and was penalized just twice, all the more reason why he was so appealing to NFL scouts.

When the Miami Dolphins selected him first, Long became the first Michigan player since Heisman Trophy winner Tom Harmon in 1941 to go No. 1. He become the second offensive lineman to be selected first since 1970, joining former Ohio State tackle Orlando Pace, who was chosen by the Rams in 1997.

NFL commissioner Roger Goodell poses with Michigan tackle Jake Long, who was selected first overall by the Miami Dolphins in the 2008 NFL Draft.

The Dolphins were so eager to have Long signed, sealed, and delivered, they settled his contract before draft day, signing him for $57.5 million over five years, including $30 million guaranteed.

"It is something I think every kid dreams about," Long said of playing professionally. "Ever since I started playing football, I dreamt about playing in the NFL and getting drafted. Coming into college, I dreamt about being the No. 1 draft pick and being one of the best players in college football. It is something I dreamed about, and I worked hard to get here."

37 Mike Hart: All-Time Leading Rusher

Mike Hart's goal as a Michigan football player was simple—he wanted only to be the best. He left Michigan as the program's all-time leading rusher with 5,040 yards, following a career that started with a bang his first season when he rushed for 1,455 yards, the most ever by a UM freshman tailback.

"Whatever I do, I don't like losing," he said. "I want to be the best."

Hart, the diminutive back who was a sixth-round NFL Draft pick by the Indianapolis Colts in 2008, was, as many would say, the "heart" of the Michigan offense that in his senior season featured left tackle Jake Long—the No. 1 overall pick in the draft—and quarterback Chad Henne.

He often was thought of as the mouth of the team, as well. In a good way, of course. His teammates frequently made fun of Hart and how much he could talk. His onetime roommate, Morgan Trent, even joked that Hart kept the conversation going long after he was asleep. Among some of his verbal highlights at Michigan:

Mike Hart stiff-arms Wisconsin defensive back Allen Langford in Ann Arbor in September 2006 during the Wolverines' 27–13 win.

guaranteeing a victory over Notre Dame after the Wolverines started the 2007 season with two losses, and referring to Michigan State later that season as Michigan's "little brother."

Hart may have rubbed some the wrong way, but he was a leader among his teammates. He was voted, along with Long and linebacker Shawn Crable, a team captain his senior season. It was his ability to literally rally the team, not to mention his ability as a hard-nosed runner, that appealed to his coaches.

"That's why he's one of the best football players to ever wear that uniform," said Lloyd Carr, Hart's head coach.

He entered his senior season as a Heisman Trophy hopeful, but a high ankle sprain slowed him during the fall. Still, he started that season believing he was the best back in the country, even though he knew he was not a big-play back and didn't have gaudy yards from long runs. He believed he was a complete back, perhaps the most versatile in the game that season. He was terrific in pass-blocking situations, a job he prided himself on; he was mistake free—he had only three fumbles in his career including two in his final game, the Capital One Bowl against Florida on New Year's Day 2008; he was incredibly competitive and would not allow himself to be out-worked; and when he ran the ball, he never let his legs stop, allowing him to gain yards after initial contact.

"That's just determination," Hart said.

He was, ultimately, the total package: consistent and tough.

"There might be someone faster than me, there might be someone stronger than me, there might be someone quicker than me, there might be someone who can catch better than me," Hart said. "I can do everything."

During his senior season, Hart began signing autographs "H20."

"Smooth," he said. "Runs like water."

And for the most yards in Michigan history.

38 2000: The Michigan-Alabama Orange Bowl

What a way for Michigan to kick off the new millennium.

The Wolverines twice erased 14-point deficits to beat Alabama 35–34 in the program's first overtime game, on January 1, 2000. Michigan was ranked No. 8 and Alabama No. 5 entering the post-season matchup.

Alabama kicker Ryan Pflugner missed an extra-point attempt wide right after what was the Crimson Tide's apparent game-tying touchdown.

"I knew it was going to go right," Pflugner said after the game, "but I didn't know it was going to be that far right."

"I hated to see it end the way it did, because I feel bad for that kicker," Michigan coach Lloyd Carr said at the time. "But...I thought we deserved to win."

Michigan quarterback Tom Brady played memorably and completed 34 of 46 passes for 369 yards and four touchdowns. Three of those touchdown passes went to David Terrell. Brady, like most of the Wolverines, fought exhaustion late in the game.

Before Michigan's final drive in regulation—a drive that ended when Hayden Epstein's 36-yard field-goal attempt was blocked by Alabama safety Phillip Weeks—Brady, who was dehydrated, threw up on the sideline.

"When guys are counting on you, it doesn't matter what it takes," Brady said after the game. "It wasn't just me. Every guy, all the linemen, everyone was dog tired out there."

Brady threw to eight different receivers, including tight end Shawn Thompson, who scored on the first play of Michigan's first overtime on a 25-yard pass. That touchdown gave Michigan its first lead of the game at 35–28.

Terrell and Alabama running back Shaun Alexander were major forces for their teams during regulation, but neither played much of a role in overtime. After Brady and Thompson connected for the Michigan score, Alexander set up an Alabama score with a four-yard run. Antonio Carter caught a 21-yard pass from Andrew Zow for the score. Then Pflugner pushed his extra-point attempt wide right.

Terrell had career bests in receiving yards (150) and receiving touchdowns (three) and equaled his career high in receptions (10). He was named the Orange Bowl MVP. Brady threw for a Michigan bowl–record 369 yards.

This was the third meeting between Michigan and Alabama, all in bowl-game settings, and each game came down to the final seconds. The Wolverines beat Alabama 28–24 on a fourth-down touchdown pass in the final minute of the 1988 Hall of Fame Bowl, and in the 1997 Outback Bowl the Crimson Tide scored two touchdowns in the fourth quarter for a 17–14 comeback victory.

39 The Game 1997: A Perfect End to the Dream Season

When the game had ended—Michigan's 11–0 regular season intact with a 20–14 win over archrival Ohio State—the Wolverines ran onto the Michigan Stadium field with red roses in their hands, and some, like Charles Woodson, clenched the roses between their teeth. This was, in simplistic terms, Michigan's dream season. Before a Michigan Stadium–record 106,982, the Wolverines maintained their No. 1 ranking and clinched a berth in the Rose Bowl after a five-year absence.

"It was their determination, more than anything else, to have a great season," their coach, Lloyd Carr, later said. "They won because they had the resolve to win."

This game showcased the Wolverines' remarkable two-way player, Charles Woodson, who weeks later would become the first primarily defensive player to win the Heisman Trophy. Woodson led a defense that would come up big in the end, holding down a no-quit Ohio State team that wanted nothing more than to do what the Wolverines had done to the Buckeyes before—spoil the perfect season.

With Michigan's offense untracked when tailback Chris Howard left the game after the first half because of a concussion, the defense, dominant all season with end Glen Steele anchoring a tough front four, forced three turnovers and had five sacks.

"This was my dream—to go undefeated, beat Ohio State at home, and go to the Rose Bowl," said safety Marcus Ray, ironically, a Columbus, Ohio, native. "That's why I came here, that's why my teammates came here, too."

Woodson shined. He returned a punt 78 yards for a touchdown and briefly considered striking the Heisman Trophy pose as Michigan receiver Desmond Howard had done in the 1991 OSU game but was too quickly mobbed by his teammates. He also caught a 37-yard pass that led to the game's first score, intercepted a pass in the end zone, and largely shut down David Boston, who had chirped before the game that the Buckeyes would win by several touchdowns. Woodson broke up a pass and had three tackles, wrapping up a day that wrapped up the Heisman Trophy.

Freshman Anthony Thomas gave UM their first score and a 7–0 lead on a one-yard run. Woodson added to that on the 78-yard punt return late in the second quarter, but Kraig Baker's extra-point attempt was blocked. Michigan carried a 13–0 lead into halftime.

Woodson prevented an OSU touchdown on the opening drive of the second half when he intercepted Stanley Jackson's pass intended for Dee Miller in the end zone.

"I just cut underneath the pass, and Stanley Jackson threw me a great pass," Woodson said.

Michigan's lead grew to 20–0 with 10:29 left in the game when Andre Weathers intercepted a pass from Jackson and returned it 43 yards for the touchdown.

The Buckeyes, however, fought back from that deficit. Boston beat Woodson for a 56-yard touchdown pass from Joe Germaine with 4:50 left. Boston backpedaled the final four yards while taunting Woodson.

Later, Ray said the Wolverines were happy the Buckeyes still had something left. "This was the kind of game we wanted," Ray said. "We wanted a dogfight for the championship."

And it was.

The Buckeyes closed the gap to 20–14 when quarterback Brian Griese made his only mistake of the game, a fumble deep in Michigan territory. He had been blindsided by Gary Berry, and the fumble was recovered and returned to the 2-yard line by Jerry Rudzinski. Pepe Pearson scored on the next play.

"We knew that the game was basically on our shoulders, and if we wanted to go back to the Rose Bowl, then we had to come up big," Woodson said.

Three times the Buckeyes had the ball in the fourth quarter with a chance to win, and three times the Michigan defense held, thanks mostly to the play of the front four. Germaine and the Buckeyes were denied a first down on their last two possessions. Steele had two sacks in the final four minutes.

"We knew we'd get 'em stopped because someone always comes up with a big play," linebacker Sam Sword said. "There was no denying us the summit. The air gets thin at the top, but when you get that close, there's no turning back."

Michigan, which played without Chris Howard in the second half and without starting left tackle Jeff Backus, out with a reinjured right ankle, finished with 189 yards of offense.

40 The 1994 Colorado Game: A Painful Hail Mary

It isn't a game Michigan fans want to remember, but certainly it is one that's difficult to forget. The No. 4 Wolverines looked to have their third straight victory of 1994 in the bag with six seconds remaining, but seventh-ranked Colorado had a plan. Buffaloes quarterback Kordell Stewart scrambled in the pocket and then heaved a 64-yard Hail Mary on the game's final play that was tipped by Blake Anderson and into the hands of Detroit-native Michael Westbrook in the end zone, as the Buffaloes silenced the Michigan Stadium crowd with the stunning 27–26 victory.

Michigan players stood on the field and on the sideline in disbelief, uncertain of what they had just witnessed.

"It was like, 'This didn't really happen, did it?'" Chuck Winters said in an interview several years later. "We all just sat around [in the locker room] and looked at each other, like, 'Man, did this really just happen?'"

Winters had a good look at the play, named "Rocket Left." The same play had been called to end the first half, but Winters made the interception.

"So," Winters later said, "we knew that Stewart could throw it that far."

Westbrook wasn't the intended receiver on the play. Because he stood 6'4", his job was to outleap everyone and try to tip the ball to a teammate. That's not how it played out, though. Winters would later reveal he had the ball in his hands, but Anderson leaped up and tipped it away. Westbrook went diving for the ball and cradled it, as he dragged Michigan cornerback Ty Law for the touchdown and the upset. Michigan had led by 12 points with two and a half minutes left.

"I had the ball in my hands," Winters said. "I tipped it...it bounced off my hand."

Stewart's pass actually traveled 73 yards.

"Only a guy with Kordell's ability could throw that far...and stay alive to throw that far," Colorado coach Bill McCartney, a former Michigan assistant, said after the game. "I didn't think he could throw it that far."

Stewart, with tears in his eyes, kissed the grass in the end zone. Meanwhile, Westbrook taunted the Michigan crowd, yelling at them to "Give it up!"

Winters many years later replayed the scene for Jim Brandstatter in his book, *Tales from Michigan Stadium*. "The key at the end of the game, all of our underneath guys missed jamming the receivers at the line of scrimmage," Winters said. "So I'm backing up and we've got Westbrook, [Rae] Carruth, and another guy coming down on us. I'm running with the third guy, and I've got him covered. Ty Law is running with Westbrook, and he's trailing by just a little.

"When the ball goes up, we're all in position, and Ty tries to intercept it. As we jumped, both of us got hit in the legs and thrown off balance. The ball bounced of Ty's shoulder pads, and as I'm falling, I can see Westbrook right behind me catching the ball. That was the worst feeling in the world right there. We were just sick. It took me at least two weeks to get over it."

With 5:08 left in the game and Colorado trailing 26–14, Stewart fumbled at the Michigan goal line. The Buffaloes managed to hold the Wolverines and then drove 72 yards in 1:36, and Rashaan Salaam scored on a one-yard run to make it 26–21.

The Wolverines recovered the onside kick with just more than two minutes left, but they had to punt with 21 seconds left, leaving 15 seconds for Colorado to go 85 yards. Westbrook caught a pass from Stewart at the Colorado 36, and then Stewart spiked the ball to kill the clock with six seconds remaining.

McCartney later called it "the ultimate victory."

41 Bentley Historical Library

For those who are interested in researching the history of Michigan football and for those who simply want to spend time sifting through historical records, or even the boxes of correspondence and clipping and notes that were once kept by legendary coach Fritz Crisler, the Bentley Historical Library is the place to go.

The Bentley, as it is often referred to, is located on Michigan's North Campus and is open without fee to any and all researchers. It is a remarkable place with an even more remarkable collection of all things related to Michigan football.

Like most libraries, the Bentley has normal sign-in procedures, and the average fan not necessarily interested in research can walk in and inform the archivists what it is he or she is looking for. The library keeps hours on Saturday mornings from 9:00 AM to 12:30 PM, and fans headed to home football games often drop by.

"I think that anybody who is going to do any serious Michigan football research should come here," said Greg Kinney, the Bentley Library's associate archivist. "Compared to some schools, I have talked to some researchers at universities across the country, and they all generally say the Michigan athletics department has a sense of its own history, and they had foresight to transfer it to us and put it in one place. This is a place to do research."

While this is *the* place for serious Michigan football researchers, who have been known to spend an awful lot of time at the Bentley, it is equally as welcoming to the casual or serious fan who simply wants to do some poking through history.

"Probably most of our people are just casual fans, and they want to look at stuff," Kinney said. "A lot of the interest is in genealogical things. People come in and say, 'Oh, my grandfather played at Michigan,' and they want to look that up."

Often, former players stop in. Surprisingly, many don't have photographs of themselves from their playing days, and they make copies of those from the Bentley files. A lot of alums, Kinney said, like to see football programs from the games they attended while in school. The library has an enormous collection of vintage programs—many of the covers from programs through the mid-'30s have been scanned, while the originals are in storage.

Kinney said most of the research requests are fairly typical, but he has received one that may or may not have been a marriage deal-breaker. "The strangest request I ever had: a woman from Texas called, and she was going to surprise her fiancé with a team photo," Kinney said. "She said he told her he had played for Bo [Schembechler], but as far as we could tell through our research, he didn't play here, and there was no record indicating he went to school here."

The Bentley also serves the Internet crowd, having gone online at www.bentley.umich.edu. There are terrific online databases, like the all-time football database. You can type in any player name, and it will link to information about that player. There's also an interesting database devoted to the artwork from game-day programs.

42 The Story of the Maize and Blue

Everyone knows Michigan's colors are maize and blue. But colors are tricky, and because there a variety of shades and hues, is it really as simple as yellow and blue?

Graphic designer Liene Karels did considerable research on the subject matter for *Michigan Today* in 1996, and she came up with a long history of how the colors became associated with Michigan.

She found that the first recorded association of any color with Michigan was on the 1859 diploma belonging to Elisha Jones. A deep-blue ribbon was attached to the diploma. A committee of University of Michigan students was appointed in 1867 to come up with colors that would symbolize and represent the school. Later that year, the students offered their report:

"Your committee, appointed to select emblematic colors for our University, unanimously agree in presenting as their choice,

Azure Blue and Maize, and recommend that the following resolution be adopted: Resolved that Azure Blue and Maize be adopted as the emblematic colors of the University of Michigan."

The resolution passed, but because colors vary, Michigan's colors started to range from dark blue to sky blue to pale yellow and lemon. But in the early 1900s, the Michigan Athletic Association unofficially adopted its own shades, going with deep blue and bright yellow for team uniforms, while the rest of the university used more of the pale colors. In 1912, seeing that colors used for diploma ribbons and robes and official documents all appeared somewhat different, the University Senate developed another committee, chaired by Dr. W.P. Lombard, to settle on the exact shades of the University colors. Specific shades of maize and azure blue were selected…again.

But Lombard's work was not done. The committee was also requested to "embody [the colors] in some lasting form." What did that mean, exactly? For Lombard, it meant commissioning enamels from artisans in New York and Norway to match the selected colors, but remarkably no one could guarantee an exact match. So the committee settled on broad grosgrain ribbons to provide the exact colors.

Karels, in 1996, decided that she would capture the official maize and blue colors in a permanent form. She found, as did her predecessors 80 years earlier, that finding exact replication of colors from original fabric samples that had faded and deteriorated would be difficult. A company in Grandville, Michigan—X-Rite Incorporated—used its technology for precise color measurement to help Karels in her quest. The company helped determine the University's true colors.

Every football fan, however, knows the team's colors. The Wolverines wear maize pants for home and away games, and their home jersey is dark blue with maize numerals, while the away jersey is white with blue numerals piped in maize.

The school song, "The Yellow and Blue," does not mention maize or azure, but the point certainly comes across in its final verse:
"Here's to the college whose colors we wear,
Here's to the hearts that are true!
Here's to the maid of the golden hair,
And eyes that are brimming with blue!
Garlands of bluebells and maize intertwine,
And hearts that are true and voices combine;
Hail! Hail to the college whose colors we wear;
Hurrah for the Yellow and Blue!"

43 The Great Reality of the Fantasy Camp

For $5,000 you, too, can be a Michigan Wolverines. Well, sort of. You can dress at a locker bearing your name, wear the famed winged helmet, and don a blue home jersey with your name emblazoned across the shoulders.

So even a decade, two, or three (or more) after your college years are complete, being a Michigan football player can be a reality.

If you have the financial resources—it might make the check writing more palatable knowing that the majority of the fee goes to the "Men of Michigan" prostate cancer research fund at the University of Michigan Hospital—participating in the fantasy camp is a can't-miss opportunity. The camp had been on hiatus for four years before Brady Hoke and his staff resumed hosting it in 2012.

For two days, the male fantasy campers (there is a one-day camp for women) live, breathe, and eat Michigan football in an atmosphere as close to authentic as possible.

Women Go Camping

While Michigan offers a two-day camp for its male fans to "live" like Wolverines players and learn from the coaching staff, Michigan's female fans also have a similar opportunity.

The Women's Football Academy was launched in 1999 as the primary fund-raiser for the Coach Carr Cancer Fund, an endowment fund established by Lloyd and Laurie Carr to support patient care and wellness programs at the UM Comprehensive Cancer Center.

The annual event, carried on after Carr's retirement by Michigan coaches Rich Rodriguez and Brady Hoke, is held in mid-June and is open to 500 women each year. This gives women—and by the way, knowing football is not a requirement—a chance to understand the game by working with the head coach and his staff. Participants learn about offense, defense, and special-team strategies, skills, and techniques, and they go through practice drills and end the day with a scrimmage.

Registration typically is $100, $25 of which is tax deductible. For more information, visit http://umccc.kintera.org/faf/home/.

For two days, they are Michigan football players, taking in a team meeting in the Schembechler Hall team meeting room, reviewing practice film, and going through practice drills with the Michigan football staff.

The campers, who spend the night at a local Ann Arbor hotel, get up early the second day and prepare for practice. The camp offers an intense, behind-the-scenes look at how Michigan football players and coaches prepare. They dress in the locker room, with their names posted above their assigned lockers. And they have a pregame meal with the coaches just as the players do. They go through a full team meeting with the head coach and then they learn offensive and defensive play installations with all of the coaches. Then there's practice and more of the same the next day.

While "fantasy camp" might sound like fun and games, it truly is an intensive learning experience. Campers learn 22 positions, sit in the Schembechler Hall team meetings rooms, experience first-hand how coaches handle and instruct the players—often learning what it feels like to get yelled at—and break down game film. All in all, it's a fairly complex experience.

The campers leave with a different appreciation of Michigan football.

"It gives you a sense of what the players have to go through as far as how much they have to learn, the terminology they have to understand," said Richard Watnick, a Michigan alum and Detroit-area physician who has participated in the camp. "The best part has been watching how the coaches interact with the players on the field. How they try to inspire, motivate, how they try to intimidate."

For the campers, the highlight, of course, is leaving the locker room, lining up in the tunnel, then making their way onto the field at Michigan Stadium. This is the moment most Michigan fans dream about.

"I would have paid more if I had to," said Tom Wolfe, a Detroit-area physician and longtime Michigan football fan. "There is nothing like getting yelled at by a Michigan football coach."

44 Where Is the Michigan Mascot?

Ohio State has Brutus Buckeye, Iowa has Herky the Hawk, Wisconsin has Bucky Badger, and Northwestern has Willie the Wildcat, just to name a few of the Big Ten mascots. Michigan's nickname is the Wolverines, but why isn't there a Willie the Wolverine? Or a Wylie the Wolverine? Or even a Wolvie Wolverine?

Well, for one thing, the Michigan athletics department has always maintained that having a mascot is unnecessary, undignified, and would not reflect the spirit and values of athletics at the university. That seems to say it all, but it hasn't prevented a number of people and groups from proposing mascots with different versions of a wolverine costume, all of which have been rejected by the athletics department.

So why the Wolverines?

Michigan students and alumni began referring to the nickname as early as 1861, but that still doesn't explain why they chose the wolverine to be their representative.

Wolverines actually belong to the weasel family and are not related to the wolf, as some have believed. The animals are considered clever and resourceful and are noted for their aggressiveness and fearlessness. They are always on the move, which may explain why the first verified sighting of a wild wolverine inside the state of Michigan was in February 2004. There has never been a trapping of a wolverine within the state, nor have skeletal remains of a wolverine been found.

So again, why the Wolverines?

Legendary Michigan football coach Fielding H. Yost wrote in the *Michigan Quarterly Review* in 1944 of his theory regarding the origins of the nickname. Yost believed the source involved the trading of wolverine pelts that occurred at Sault Ste. Marie, which served as a trading exchange among Native Americans, trappers, and fur traders. Because they were wolverine pelts, the traders may have referred to them as "Michigan wolverines." Thus, the state nickname and school mascot.

About 20 years before Yost wrote of his theory, he tried to find a wolverine to have at the football games. He had been inspired by Wisconsin's team, which brought live badgers with them. Yost wrote to numerous trappers, but came up empty-handed. He finally found a mounted wolverine in the fall of 1924, but he continued to pursue locating a live animal. Three years later, the Detroit Zoo acquired 10 wolverines from Alaska, and on game days, two of those animals were transported to Michigan Stadium and carried around in cages.

A year later, that tradition ended. The wolverines had grown larger and more aggressive.

"It was obvious that the Michigan mascots had designs on the Michigan men toting them, and those designs were by no means friendly," Yost said at the time.

One of the wolverines was housed at the University of Michigan Zoo where students could visit it. In 1937 a wolverine was donated to Michigan, and a contest held to name the mascot yielded a unique name—"Intrepidus." No one, however, is certain how long Intrepidus survived.

45 Dan Dierdorf: Finally Playing for Bo

Entering the spring semester of his senior year in high school, Dan Dierdorf had received very little interest from major programs in Division I football. Suddenly, he caught a break. A player who had committed to Michigan decided to go elsewhere. Dierdorf's high school coach had grown up with Don James, the Wolverines' defensive backs coach at the time. Done deal—Dierdorf would wear maize and blue during his college career.

Miami (Ohio) University, however, was recruiting Dierdorf. He hadn't bothered to tell then–Miami coach Bo Schembechler that he was heading to Ann Arbor, so Schembechler went ahead and paid a recruiting visit to Canton, Ohio, to see Dierdorf.

"Now, I had actually made my recruiting trip to Oxford [Ohio], and I had decided that I did not want to play for Bo Schembechler," Dierdorf said. "So being the responsible, fine upstanding young man I was, I went out the back door and left him sitting there. I'm going to Ann Arbor, Michigan, he's in

Dan Dierdorf, showing affection here for his former coach, is still considered one of the greatest offensive linemen in Michigan history. Photo courtesy of Per Kjeldsen.

Oxford, Ohio. What the heck do I care? I'm never going to see him again."

Dierdorf laughs when he tells the story. After his sophomore year at Michigan, he read in the local paper that Schembechler would be the next Michigan head coach beginning with the 1969 season.

"So I figure the best defense is a good offense," Dierdorf said. "I'm going right down there, and I'm just going to welcome him to town. So I'm walking down the hallway that leads to the coaches' office, and he comes out of his office, almost as if on cue.

"I'm like, 'Coach Schembechler, how are you doing?' and stick out my hand. He sticks his hand out and his hand goes right past my hand, and he grabs me right in the stomach. He looks me in the eye and says, 'You're fat, you're mine, and I never forget.'"

Despite their rocky start, Dierdorf excelled on the offensive line under Schembechler. During his freshman season at Michigan, Dierdorf played on the offensive and defensive lines just as he had at Glenwood High.

"It wasn't my decision [to play on offense]," he said. "The starting offensive tackles my freshman year graduated before my sophomore year, but the two defensive tackles were still there. So in spring practice, the coaches worked me at offensive tackle, and I just stayed there. It's that simple. I just wanted to play football."

Dierdorf, who combined terrific strength and speed, remains one of the finest offensive tackles at Michigan and was a consensus All-American in 1970 at right tackle. In 1971 he was selected in the second round of the NFL Draft by the St. Louis Cardinals. He played in six Pro Bowls during a 13-year career.

He has been inducted into the College Football Hall of Fame and the Pro Football Hall of Fame, which was built while he was growing up, about a 10-minute walk from his Canton home.

46 Anthony Carter: Michigan's No. 1

He wore No. 1, and he was No. 1 in many statistical categories when he left Michigan after a four-year career. Anthony Carter, the skinny receiver whose quiet demeanor never matched his on-field exploits, was perhaps the greatest Michigan receiver of all-time. Carter, better known as "A.C.," held 12 major school records, from receiving yards to kickoff return yardage, by the time his career ended after the 1982 season.

Anthony Carter races to the end zone with the clock expired to score the winning touchdown over Indiana in Ann Arbor on October 27, 1979. Carter took a pass from quarterback John Wangler, stumbled, then broke a tackle and went 15 yards for the score.

The 5'11", 160-pounder from Florida was special from the start. The first time Carter touched the ball for the Wolverines as a freshman, he returned a punt 78 yards for a touchdown. Carter was hardly physically imposing, but he was elusive and quick. He was, quite literally, a threat to score every time he touched the ball.

"His body was like the last thing you draw if you wanted the perfect football body," said former Michigan quarterback John Wangler, who played with Carter. "His legs were three-quarters of his body, he had skinny little calves and a big butt, but he could go as fast sideways as he could forward. And he could go across the middle and take hits.

"Braylon [Edwards, who later broke Carter's all-time receiving yards record] was good and he was great, but he wasn't Anthony."

In his four seasons with the Wolverines—and remember, this was a Michigan offense geared more to the run but evolved with Carter—Carter averaged 17.4 yards every time he touched the ball. And as much as he was known for his receiving, Carter was equally as gifted handling kickoff and punt returns. Still, it was his touchdown-making ability as a receiver that was so breathtaking. Carter scored 37 career touchdowns, but he scored on one of every four catches.

"They dropped out of the sky, most of the them," Wangler said, laughing, clearly giving the credit to Carter's ability and not his as the quarterback.

Carter was a three-time All-American, becoming at that time only the eighth player in Big Ten history to achieve that, and was the first in 36 years. In 1980 he became the first Michigan sophomore to be named the team MVP, and after his senior season, for which he was a tri-captain, Carter was the Big Ten's Most Valuable Player and finished fourth in Heisman Trophy voting.

All of those accolades aside, Carter remained humble. In fact, he never particularly enjoyed the heat of the spotlight and was nicknamed the "hermit" by his teammates.

He was inducted into the College Football Hall of Fame in 2001.

And while his records were broken, Carter remains second in career receiving yards with 3,076, second in punt-return yardage (904), and second in kickoff-return yardage (1,606).

When Carter left Michigan in 1982, he signed a four-year, $2.1 million contract with the USFL's Michigan Panthers, for which he played three years. He then signed with the Minnesota Vikings of the NFL, where he played from 1985 to 1993, and then played two seasons with the Detroit Lions. His professional career ended after the 1995 season.

But it will always be A.C.'s college career at Michigan that will be remembered.

"Anthony was the best," Wangler said. "He was a wonderful teammate. He never wanted to be treated any differently. But he was the kind of guy, of all the great athletes on the field, you could not take your eyes off him."

47 Tom Curtis: Career Interception Leader

When Tom Curtis arrived at Michigan, he had dreams of being a quarterback. Who knew he would end up being such a huge thorn for opposing quarterbacks?

During his Hall of Fame career from 1967 to 1969—freshmen didn't play with the varsity at that time—Curtis had 25 career interceptions. That's seven more than Heisman Trophy winner Charles Woodson, who is second on the career list. That total of 25 ranks Curtis second all-time in Big Ten history and ties him for fourth in NCAA history. In 2005 he was inducted into the College Football Hall of Fame as one of the greatest interception threats in college football history.

"I look back at it and, as my mother always said, 'How did you do that, Tommy?'" Curtis said. "I still have no idea. That record stands today [at Michigan], and I only played 31 games because we weren't eligible as freshmen. We didn't play 12 games like they do now. I don't know how I did it. I wasn't strong, I wasn't fast, but I had great instincts, and I had really good hands."

Curtis was an All-America safety in 1969, set an NCAA career record with 431 interception-return yards, and led the nation with 10 interceptions in 1968, which is still a single-season Michigan record. He was a two-time All–Big Ten first-team selection, and he led the Wolverines in interceptions for three straight seasons.

It's pretty amazing, considering the native Ohioan came to Michigan as a quarterback.

"I never thought I was going to be a defensive back—I still think I should have been a quarterback," Curtis said, laughing. "I got to Michigan, and we had four quarterbacks on scholarship. There was plenty of competition.

"During spring practice my sophomore year, I won one of the safety jobs. I had success, and I never looked back."

But when he does look back, Curtis first recalls the play that didn't go his way against Navy his sophomore year.

"The Navy quarterback lobbed the pass over the middle to me, and I dropped it," Curtis said. "I didn't have an interception yet, and I had it in my hands…. I got benched the next game, but that lasted a quarter and a half, and I got back in there."

Curtis won Michigan's academic Frederic Matthaei Award in 1968 and graduated with a degree in economics in 1970. After graduation, he was drafted by the Baltimore Colts and played two seasons in the NFL. Of course, he remembers the one that Joe Namath threw to him and he dropped.

Sadly, Curtis, who is the owner and publisher of several NFL team publications, lost all of his Michigan and NFL memorabilia in a fire at his Miami office. But still, he has his memories.

"Maybe it's selfish and maybe it's wrong, but I believe Michigan is different," Curtis said. "I believe Michigan is a unique place, and I believe Michigan, for the most part, does things right. That helmet and those traditions mean something to me, and mean something to everybody who played there."

48 Michigan's Retired Numbers

Gerald Ford could not deny the honor he felt when sworn in as President of the United States in 1974, but he had to admit, having his No. 48 retired by Michigan in 1994 also was a thrill. Ford played on Michigan's national championship teams in 1932 and 1933 and was the Wolverines' Most Valuable Player in 1934. At halftime of the Michigan–Michigan State game on October 8, 1994, his number joined four others that have been retired at Michigan. Michigan has not retired a number since.

"On a personal level, this is as meaningful to me," said Ford during a teleconference with media before his jersey retirement when asked how the two events compared.

Ford, a native of Grand Rapids, Michigan, flew to Ann Arbor from his Colorado home and addressed the team before the game. He told the Wolverines "that they can and will uphold the great Michigan tradition."

Bennie Oosterbaan, the decorated multisport athlete, a three-time football All-American and former football coach at Michigan, saw his jersey No. 47 retired first.

Henry Hatch, Michigan's longtime equipment manager who worked under seven head coaches, reportedly decided that no other player would be worthy enough to wear Oosterbaan's number. "Nobody's ever going to make All-American three years running again," Hatch said after Oosterbaan's graduation in the 1920s. "I'm not going to give Bennie's number out."

Hatch was almost right. Anthony Carter was a three-time All-American at Michigan from 1980 to 1982. Still, Oosterbaan was a phenomenal college athlete and is considered one of the greatest to play for the Wolverines and one of the greatest all-around athletes in Big Ten history.

Tom Harmon, the first Michigan Heisman Trophy winner, was the last to wear No. 98. Hatch decided Harmon's jersey would be the second retired.

"The book was closed on No. 98 today, and equipment manager Henry Hatch of Michigan university put it reverently away in a musty trunk beside No. 47," according to a United Press account.

What's in a Number?

It's all in the numbers.

Being an All-American at Michigan is no easy feat, of course, but does it have something to do with the player's jersey number? Does the jersey number make the player, or is it the other way around?

If you want to be an All-American at Michigan, your best bet is to wear jersey No. 1 or No. 72. There have been five players representing both numbers that have gone on to All-America status. Those All-Americans who wore No. 1 at Michigan were Paul Goebel, Anthony Carter, Derrick Alexander, David Terrell, and Braylon Edwards. And those All-Americans who wore No. 72 were Allen Wahl, Dan Dierdorf, Walt Downing, Ed Muransky, and John Elliott.

If those are taken, try No. 75 or No. 77, both of which have been worn by four All-Americans apiece. No. 75 was worn by All-Americans William Yearby, William Paris, Greg Skrepenak, and David Baas. No. 77 was worn by Arthur Walker, Paul Seymour, Jon Jansen, and Jake Long.

Unique to Michigan and to college football, the No. 11 was worn by three brothers, the Wisterts—Francis, Albert, and Alvin. Francis Wistert had been an All-American for the Wolverines, and when Albert arrived at Michigan, jersey No. 11 was bestowed upon him by Hatch in 1940, although he had never made that request.

Ron Kramer, a two-time All-American in 1955 and 1956 and a three-sport athlete at Michigan, had his jersey No. 87 retired after his senior season.

Since Ford's jersey retirement, there have been no others—and there likely will not be. In 2011, Michigan began a new tradition with "Michigan Football Legend" patches. This way, a jersey number remains in circulation, but a "legend patch," located on the left upper chest, designates it as something special. The first recipient of this new honor? Desmond Howard, the 1991 Heisman Trophy winner, who wore No. 21.

Michigan athletic director Dave Brandon said it is possible that the five retired numbers may be put back into circulation with legend patches.

"This is a great way to honor our legends," Brandon said. "This concept is a visible representation of iconic figures in our program's storied history that fans across the country will see every Saturday."

49 The Story of the M Ring

Michigan football players past and present, although from different eras and from different parts of the country, share a common bond as part of this football fraternity. They all toiled in the weight room, on the practice field, and certainly on Saturdays. They wore the famed winged helmet, they donned the maize-and-blue colors, and they always will be known as Wolverines.

To commemorate those who played four years at Michigan, the University of Michigan Club of Detroit continues a tradition that began in 1921. Each year at the annual football banquet, the seniors are presented an M Ring.

It is simple in design but rich in tradition, and to the players, it is a lasting memory of their football careers at Michigan. The ring is gold and features a round blue enamel center with a maize block "M" in the middle of the blue field. There are no diamonds or gemstones and no gaudy design. "It is what it should be," said former offensive lineman Jim Brandstatter, color analyst on Michigan football radio broadcasts. "It's simple and classy."

When Bo Schembechler arrived as head coach in 1969, he was told the rings were presented to players who played a certain number of minutes through their four years. Schembechler immediately altered the tradition. If a player practiced and stayed four years, he would be honored with a ring at the conclusion of his career. That has since been the M Ring tradition.

"It's really an indication, a remembrance that you completed four years of football at the University of Michigan and that you contributed greatly," Brandstatter said. "It becomes a maize-and-blue badge of courage. It binds you with all those guys who came before. When you see a Ron Kramer or a Bob Chappuis wearing theirs, and you're wearing yours, you realize you're part of a fraternity that is pretty special.

"I have two Big Ten championship rings, and I'm very proud of those, but the M ring goes beyond that. Myself and [Rick] Leach and Tom Harmon and Chappuis and Julius Franks and Ron Johnson...it puts us on the same team. We played for Michigan. After the lights fade and the days you could get down in a football stance fade, those championship rings, as important as they are, the M Ring is more important because of what it stands for—the team you are a part of."

Brandstatter said he is moved every time he sees Kramer, a former two-time All-American at Michigan who went on to play for Vince Lombardi and the Green Bay Packers, wearing his M Ring. Here's a guy who, long after his Michigan days were over, created lasting NFL memories, but his jewelry of choice is his M Ring.

"To me, that says something," Brandstatter said. "To me, that's why I like to wear mine. It puts me in exclusive company. You realize you're part of a bigger team, part of a tradition of excellence. By wearing that M Ring, you're part of something special."

Lloyd Carr retired as Michigan's head coach after the 2007 season. At the football banquet that December, he became one of only two non-Michigan seniors to be presented with an M Ring. Bo Schembechler was the other.

50 Erick Anderson: The Only Butkus Award Winner

After three successful seasons with the Wolverines, Erick Anderson made a pledge to himself entering his final year. Anderson, a hard-nosed linebacker, became the first player in Michigan history to lead the team in tackles all four years. A cocaptain his senior year in 1991, he ended his career with 428 tackles, third on Michigan's all-time tackles list. Anderson also had 19 games in which he had double-digit tackles.

He was named an All-American and co–Big Ten Defensive Player of the Year his senior year, which ended with the biggest individual prize of all—the Butkus Award, annually awarded to the nation's top linebacker. Anderson was the first and only Michigan player to win that award, and lest you forget, legendary Michigan coach Fielding H. Yost *created* the linebacker position.

"I told myself I wanted to be the best linebacker there ever was at Michigan," Anderson once said. "I never told anyone, though. It might sound arrogant, but you have to know that I realize I would not have accomplished what I have without great teammates."

Anderson devoted himself to a challenging off-season weight and conditioning program before his final season.

"I can't imagine anyone meaning more to their team than Erick means to ours," said Lloyd Carr, then Michigan's defensive coordinator. "I would not trade him for anybody, and it's hard to believe anyone in the country has been as consistently outstanding."

Opposing coaches agreed with Carr's assessment.

"The heart and character of their defense comes out of Erick," Minnesota coach John Gutekunst said at the time. "If you need a big play or big hit, he gets it."

Anderson was destined, it seemed, to play football. His mother's father, Bob Nowaskey, played for the Chicago Bears and the Baltimore Colts, and his father's father, Donald Anderson, coached football in Wisconsin. His father, also named Donald Anderson, led Northwestern's receivers in 1967.

While Erick was playing at Michigan, his brother, Lars, was a quarterback at Indiana. Their younger brother, Kurt, eventually would play for the Wolverines.

"I always heard guys saying they wanted to be like Dick Butkus or Mike Singletary," Erick said. "I did not need to look for a hero to emulate. My dad had been there and knew what it took. So it became second nature to me, especially with my grandfathers. I always expected to do this. Going to college on a scholarship and someday playing in the NFL all seemed like something I should do."

During his senior season at Glenbrook South High in Illinois, Anderson also played on offense and rushed for 1,263 yards. But he always had a defensive mentality and approach to the game.

Anderson was known for being a complete package at linebacker. He liked hitting, he loved the contact, and he had terrific instincts. He was tough, competitive, and rarely got beat.

Also while at Michigan, Anderson took drama classes to help him overcome his shyness when it came to doing interviews with the media before and after games. He even participated in theater productions while in school with teammates Shawn Miller and Chris Stapleton.

51 LaMarr Woodley: The Only Lombardi Award Winner

LaMarr Woodley was long on talent and goofing around. Woodley was a star in high school in Saginaw, Michigan, and the state's best player. There was no doubt what kind of player he would become in high school, but coupled with that playing ability was his fondness for joking around and having fun. He maintained that demeanor through college at Michigan, where he was a dominant defensive end—that is, until he was named the defensive captain in 2006. Suddenly, with that kind of responsibility, Woodley took on a whole new role.

"You don't get another chance to do this again," Woodley said at the time. "How do you leave our last year, that's how you're going to be remembered, and that's how you're going to remember your life when you go back and look. Your last year in college, how did you finish? I wanted to leave on a positive note."

He finished on an individual high note, tying the single-season school record of 12 sacks during the 2006 season. Woodley was named Big Ten Defensive Player of the Year and Defensive Lineman of the Year. He led the Big Ten and ranked seventh nationally in sacks his final season. He also ranked fifth nationally with four forced fumbles.

Then, of course, there was the big prize, the Lombardi Award, given to the best offensive or defensive lineman in the country. Woodley was dazzled by his competition for the award—Penn State linebacker Paul Posluszny, Ohio State defensive tackle Quinn Pitcock, and Texas offensive guard Justin Blalock—and didn't believe he stood a chance.

Woodley, the first Michigan player to win the Lombardi, did not have any comments prepared when his name was called.

"I definitely was surprised," Woodley said at the time. "I was shocked. I was like, 'Oh, man.' I didn't have a speech ready. I didn't expect it at all. I never expected to win."

Also that day, he earned the Ted Hendricks Award, given to the top defensive end for on-field performance, leadership abilities, and contributions to his school and community.

He arrived at Michigan in 2003 as the state's No. 1 high school player, having starred at Saginaw High. The following year,

Woodley played at linebacker and defensive end, as the coaching staff tried to find where he fit best. In 2005, until he fractured his forearm, Woodley had been a dominant defensive force for the Wolverines the first half of the season.

"For LaMarr, it was hard for him to handle an injury like that because I've never seen him hurt in my life like that," Jerome Jackson, Woodley's teammate at Saginaw and at Michigan, said at the time. "To see him in that pain, not playing, it kind of hurt me because I've never seen him like that before."

Before his senior year, as he became accustomed to his new title of cocaptain, Woodley reset his goals. He wanted to leave Michigan with the single-season sack record that David Bowens set in 1996.

"It's definitely one of the goals, just to be remembered in the Michigan tradition and Michigan history," Woodley said then. "Every year I said I was going to break [the sack record], and this is the closest that I actually got to it."

52 Steve Breaston: Return Specialist

In person, Steve Breaston was quiet, thoughtful, and subtle. On the football field, he could be electrifying, not only as a receiver, but as a kick-return specialist who made opposing coaches ridiculously nervous.

It was tough to tell what made him more unique—his ability to write short stories and poetry that would dazzle because of their profound nature, or his ability to make big plays for the Wolverines, which also affected games in a profound way.

Deeply influenced by the comic books he had read as a youngster, he began to write in junior high school while growing up in

Steve Breaston (15) and Jason Avant (8) celebrate Michigan's 38–30 win over Florida in the Outback Bowl on January 1, 2003, in Tampa, Florida.

Woodland Hills, Pennsylvania. Breaston, who redshirted his first year at Michigan in 2002, wrote throughout his college career and even had one of his poems submitted for a Hopwood Award, one of the most prestigious writing honors at the university. He would always say that writing allowed him a chance to think through all the daydreams he had about life. Breaston said he sometimes would picture himself as someone else while he wrote, developing perspectives from that other point of view.

Perhaps not surprisingly, he never wrote about football.

"You're around football all the time," he later said. "I like to write about life and certain issues in my community. It's a way to express yourself, and I'm good at it and more confident with it."

During his football career, Breaston frequently dealt with injuries, but as with his writing, he also become more confident as a football player during his Michigan career.

He left Michigan as the Big Ten's career leader in punt-return yardage (1,599 yards), and his 1,993 kickoff-return yards placed him fifth in conference history. He joined Wisconsin's Nick Davis as the only players in Big Ten history to amass 1,000 career yards in three different categories.

Breaston distinguished himself at Michigan, as the career record-holder in total returns, punt returns, and kick returns. He tied a school record with four punt returns for touchdowns. He also gained more than 1,300 all-purpose yards in each of his four seasons and had seven career games with at least 200 all-purpose yards, including his brilliant Rose Bowl performance against Texas in 2005 when he had a bowl-record 315 yards.

Breaston, the 2003 Big Ten co–Freshman of the Year, was a four-year letter-winner at Michigan and made 25 starts at wide receiver. During his career, he had 156 catches for 1,696 yards and 10 touchdowns.

What made him special as a receiver is probably what set him apart as a returner.

"It was his ability to make things happen after the catch," said teammate and running back Mike Hart.

There's no doubt Breaston, who prided himself on having great vision and anticipation when it came to kick returns, was slippery, agile, and so quick, defenders would have fits. But it was Breaston's play in the 2005 Rose Bowl that was unforgettable. He had been slowed during the regular season by foot and hand injuries, but against Texas, he was back to form. His 315 all-purpose yards broke O.J. Simpson's Rose Bowl record of 276 yards in 1969. Most of Breaston's yardage came from kickoff returns. He had six for 221 yards, including a long run of 53 yards.

"He showed us what kind of athlete he is," Michigan coach Lloyd Carr said after that game.

Perhaps his biggest play of that Rose Bowl was a 50-yard touchdown reception from Chad Henne.

"He's a smooth route runner, and I see talent in him," then–Texas defensive coordinator Greg Robinson said of Breaston, now a standout in the NFL with the Kansas City Chiefs.

53 Michigan–Michigan State "Clockgate"

There have been memorable Michigan–Michigan State games, and definitely controversial Michigan–Michigan State games, but the 2001 game at Spartan Stadium took the clock…er…cake.

It now is known as "Clockgate." Michigan State won 26–24 on November 3, 2001, in dramatic, controversial fashion. The Spartans lined up, and quarterback Jeff Smoker spiked the ball on the 2-yard line with a second on the clock, giving them one final shot at the end zone.

Smoker was working from the shotgun with five receivers, including bruising, 250-pound tailback T.J. Duckett, spread wide. Smoker rolled to his right and considered running but looked for a receiver. Duckett had cut over the middle into the middle of the end zone. He appeared to almost beg for the ball before Smoker found him and lobbed him the game-winning score.

"I just heard the crowd go crazy," said Smoker, who got hit on the play and didn't see the catch.

The Wolverines were incensed.

Michigan State had spiked the ball to stop the clock with 17 seconds left at the Michigan 7-yard line. On second-and-goal, Smoker scrambled and was tackled in bounds at the 2, so the clock continued to run. With time running out, the Spartans frantically lined up to spike the ball, which they did, leaving one second left on the stadium clock.

Michigan coaches and players argued that the clock should have expired. Replays showed one second on the clock when MSU snapped the ball for Smoker to spike. Michigan radio broadcasters Jim Brandstatter and play-by-play man Frank Beckmann were memorable in their call of the final seconds.

At one point, Beckmann shouted, "That's criminal!"

"Frank has been chastised over the years for 'That's criminal!' and that truly was a great call," Brandstatter said. "It truly is hilarious and a great call."

But was it criminal?

"Oh, sure, yeah," Brandstatter said. "Now every time I see a game where a quarterback sets up and grabs the snap and spikes the ball, I look at the clock, and every game, a second or two will go off the clock before the referee signal. This clock [at Spartan Stadium] didn't move from the second before he took the snap.

"[Smoker] took the snap with one second left, he spiked it, and there was still one left. These rivalry games create all kinds of these legends. It's just like the plays players make in Michigan–Michigan State are bigger than plays made against Indiana. Things stick with people when it comes to those rivalry games."

Michigan fans agreed with Beckmann and Brandstatter, and the rest of the Michigan football team, for that matter, although the Wolverines never publically criticized the officiating. Some contend that Spartan Stadium clock operator Bob Stehlin, affectionately known at MSU as "Spartan Bob," stopped the clock before the spike play had concluded to give the Spartans a home-field clock advantage.

Former MSU coach George Perles reportedly said after the game, which he watched from the press box, "Well, I guess Spartan Bob earned a game ball today." Perles in 2008, the week of the annual in-state rivalry game, sheepishly admitted he did say that.

Lloyd Carr, then Michigan's coach, clearly was angry after the game but said little. "I'm very proud of the effort they gave," Carr said. "They deserve better."

Better from an officiating standpoint? he was asked. "They deserve better," he repeated, tersely.

Did the Wolverines feel cheated? "They deserve better," Carr said, a third time.

Carr did not indicate after the game whether he would ask for an apology from the Big Ten officials. "I'm sure the Big Ten will do the right thing, but it's not going to change the outcome," Carr said.

The following year, thanks to "Clockgate" the NCAA started to keep official time on the field.

54 Anthony Thomas: Michigan's A-Train

Fortunately for Michigan fans, Anthony Thomas' first experience with snow during a recruiting visit to Ann Arbor didn't affect him. Well, not too much.

Thomas, a tailback from Winnfield, Louisiana, was used to the hot, sticky New Orleans weather, not the frigid temperatures and snow that make Michigan winters so tough to handle. When he returned to Louisiana after that visit, he began to waffle and wondered whether playing for the Wolverines would be worth putting his body through the long winters. His family and friends told him to forget about Michigan, that he couldn't possibly play in cold weather. Suddenly, he found renewed inspiration to be a Wolverine.

"Once somebody puts a challenge to me, I try to accept that challenge and try to see what I can do," Thomas said, explaining that he wanted to prove wrong those doubting friends and family members.

Good thing he accepted that challenge, because he made the most of his four-year Michigan career in which he became known as the

"A-Train," a nickname coined by ABC announcer Brent Musburger. Thomas was a power back, a direct, powerful runner who frequently dragged defenders as he gained yards after initial contact.

Upon completion of his final season in 2000, Thomas was the Wolverines' all-time leading rusher with 4,472 yards, breaking Jamie Morris' record of 4,392 (1984–1987). Thomas' record remained intact until Mike Hart broke that mark in 2007, totaling 5,040 yards.

Thomas rushed for 1,733 yards and 18 touchdowns his senior season, and during his junior year in 1999, he rushed for 1,297 yards and scored 17 touchdowns. For his career, Thomas averaged 4.8 yards a carry and scored 55 touchdowns.

Then–Michigan coach Lloyd Carr called Thomas one of the best backs in the country and added that he was not appreciated enough for all the things he did without the ball, namely his pass protection and pass-catching ability.

While he played large on the field, Thomas was extremely quiet off the field. He didn't think much of doing interviews with the media, and his teammates frequently mentioned how little Thomas liked to talk. Not that he wasn't friendly; he just didn't talk much.

Thomas set Michigan's career record for rushing touchdowns with 55, but he never thought much about statistics or records. During his senior season, he rushed for 100 yards or more in nine of the 12 games he started, including six of 150 yards or more, a school record.

As a senior, Thomas was a Doak Walker Award finalist, All–Big Ten first team, and the Wolverines' Most Valuable Player. He ranked fifth nationally in rushing that season, averaging 141 yards, was 13th in all-purpose yards (162.73 per game), and tied for 14th in scoring (9.27 points per game).

Fortunately for Michigan fans, they got another year to watch Thomas do what he did best. He returned to college football for his final season, avoiding the lure of the NFL Draft. It certainly didn't matter to Thomas that his more talkative teammates, quarterback Drew Henson and receiver David Terrell, drew so much attention. He was a grinder, after all.

"I didn't come back for the publicity," Thomas said at the time, adding he simply wanted to win games and earn a degree.

The great irony is that as quiet as Thomas was away from football, his play was loud on the field. He wasn't the most exciting back—he wasn't flashy and was just as excited about picking up a blitzing linebacker in pass protection as he was about grinding out a yard or two on a pivotal fourth-down conversion.

Carr called Thomas the most "unassuming kid" he had ever coached.

"You would be hard-pressed to find anybody to say anything negative about him," Carr said. "And the best thing is, with all the wonderful things that he's accomplished, he hasn't changed one bit."

Rick Leach: The First Freshman to Start at QB

When the question—who is your favorite Michigan player?—is posed, frequently, the answer is Rick Leach, the phenomenally gifted, four-year starting, left-handed quarterback who wore No. 7.

Leach, a starter under Bo Schembechler from 1975 through 1978, is considered one of Michigan's finest athletes, a rare two-sport standout in the modern era who was an All-American in football and baseball.

But it was his days wearing the winged helmet for the Wolverines' football team that most fans embrace and recall. He was an extremely elusive runner and a gifted passer. Three times

Four-year starter Rick Leach is still considered by fans to be one of Michigan's all-time favorite players. Photo courtesy of Per Kjeldsen.

he was named All–Big Ten first-team quarterback, three times he placed in Heisman Trophy voting, including a third-place finish his senior season, and after that final season, he was voted Michigan's Most Valuable Player as well as the Big Ten's.

Leach, after throwing a costly interception in a loss to Ohio State his freshman year, was never again part of a losing effort against the Buckeyes. He helped lead the Wolverines to three straight Rose Bowl appearances, and in 1979 he was voted the bowl game's co–Most Valuable Player.

During his Michigan career, Leach set numerous records, among them the season record for touchdown passes (17), and he broke Big Ten records for total offense (6,460) and total touchdown passes (48). Leach also set an NCAA record for most touchdowns accounted for with 82.

Leach, who won the Big Ten batting championship as a junior and was a first-round draft selection by the Detroit Tigers in 1979, was 38–8–2 during his football career.

While in high school at Flint Southwestern High, Leach became one of the most famous athletes in Michigan high school history. He established himself in the early 1970s as a three-sport All-State athlete, starring in football, baseball, and basketball. His biggest decision upon graduation in 1975 was which sport he would play in college.

Schembechler made that easy and informed Leach he could play baseball in addition to football. But first and foremost, Leach would be the starting quarterback. And that was an amazing feat, in a sense, because he had never run the option.

"I've never seen a kid like this in my life—never," Schembechler once said of Leach. "You have to tell him only one time, and he gets it. One time."

Leach was surprised, but not shocked, when he was given the starting job for the 1975 season opener at Wisconsin. Schembechler was mum that week because he didn't want Leach to get nervous, but Leach had a hunch, considering he had been working with the first team most of the week.

"Bo still wanted to make sure I was calm as could be," Leach said, looking back.

Schembechler would later say that he decided the day before the Wolverines played at Wisconsin in 1975 that Leach would be the Wolverines' starter. "We were working out that afternoon," he said, "and I walked that young man across the field and told him, 'Son, you are starting Saturday afternoon against Wisconsin.' That's how I gave that youngster the job."

Leach helped lead the Wolverines to a 23–6 victory in that game at Camp Randall Stadium.

By the end of his freshman year, Leach had helped lead Michigan to an 8–1–2 record and a second-place finish in the Big Ten behind Ohio State.

The following year, Michigan was considered the preseason No. 1 team, and the Wolverines jumped out to an 8–0 start, playing a hard-nosed running offense and a stifling defense. They stumbled at Purdue, but came back to win the Big Ten championship by beating Ohio State in Columbus 22–0, the first of Leach's three straight victories over the hated rivals. It was later, in a 14–6 Rose Bowl loss to USC, that Schembechler decided Michigan needed to develop a passing attack and Leach would have to throw more.

Leach showed off his arm the following year and threw for 1,348 yards and 15 touchdowns. He directed big wins over then–No. 5 Texas A&M and a second straight victory over Ohio State that clinched another Rose Bowl berth. Michigan trailed 24–0 to Washington in the third quarter, but Leach, running the passing attack, began the comeback. He threw for a career-best 239 yards and had cut the deficit to 27–20 with less than two minutes left. Michigan was at the UW 8-yard line when Leach threw to tailback Stanley Jackson. The ball went through his hands and bounced off his helmet, and the pass was intercepted at the 1-yard line.

Despite the loss, Leach entered his senior season as a Heisman Trophy candidate. He and the Wolverines would have an early chance to stake their national claims with a nonconference game against defending national champion Notre Dame in the renewal of a rivalry that had taken a 35-year hiatus. Leach, however, suffered an ankle sprain early that week in practice and was held out the rest of the week. Backup B.J. Dickey practiced.

"Leach was out," Schembechler later recalled, punctuating the word "out."

At Michigan, like most schools, if a player misses practices, especially Tuesday and Wednesday, he typically won't play that Saturday. Leach played. The Wolverines defeated the Joe Montana–led Fighting Irish 28–14 in a comeback. Michigan would win a third straight against Ohio State that year, with Leach throwing two touchdowns in the 14–3 victory. Schembechler, in uncharacteristic form since Michigan has never promoted Heisman Trophy candidates, endorsed Leach, calling him the country's best player.

"If he doesn't win the Heisman award, I will be very much surprised," Schembechler said at the time. "He is the greatest player I have ever been associated with."

Leach finished third in Heisman voting.

56 Jim Harbaugh: Living and Dying with UM

These days, more than two decades after Jim Harbaugh quarterbacked Michigan with bravado and skill, his former teammates sing his praises, lauding him for his leadership and toughness, not to mention an air of cockiness and a competitive spirit that set him apart.

Harbaugh grew up in Ann Arbor, and although he spent his final two years in high school in California, Michigan already had become part of his DNA. His father, Jack, was an assistant under Bo Schembechler from 1973 to 1979, and Jim attended all the practices and even served as a ball boy.

"I lived and died with Michigan," Harbaugh has said.

Schembechler, the legendary coach, often told the story about how when he and Jack Harbaugh had returned one day to the football offices, 12-year-old Jim Harbaugh was found leaning back in Schembechler's chair with his feet up on the desk.

Harbaugh, who idolized Michigan quarterback Rick Leach, was destined to play for the Wolverines. He was a three-year starter at Michigan, from 1984 through 1986, was an All-American, Big Ten Player of the Year, and the Wolverines' Most Valuable Player as a senior. He finished third in the Heisman Trophy voting, just as Leach had.

He was known as a risk-taker and a perfectionist who sometimes let that competitive spirit take too deep a hold. Harbaugh

Guaranteeing a Win

What speaks to Michigan's lore more than quarterback Jim Harbaugh's gutsy bravado when he declared the week of the 1986 Michigan–Ohio State game that the Wolverines would beat the Buckeyes, at Ohio Stadium, no less?

While speaking to reporters at the weekly Monday luncheon to preview the next game, Harbaugh, whose team had won every game before losing to Minnesota the Saturday before, made his bold statement.

"I guarantee we'll beat Ohio State and be in Pasadena New Year's Day," Harbaugh said. "People might not give us a snowball's chance in hell to beat them in Columbus, but we're going to. We don't care where we play the game. I hate to say it, but we could play on the parking lot. We could play at 12:00 noon or midnight. We're going to be jacked up, and we're going to win."

Surprisingly, there were no angry theatrics or comments from coach Bo Schembechler. He later told his players what Harbaugh said, and it was their charge to back him up.

"The way…Bo Schembechler handled it was genius," Harbaugh said recently. "He just came into the team meeting, and I'm kind of expecting to get an earful. He said, 'Well, at least I know our quarterback thinks we can win. Rally around him. Let's go to Columbus and beat the Buckeyes.'"

And that's what Michigan did. Harbaugh threw for 261 yards and directed an offense that gained 529 to win 26–24.

demanded as much from his teammates, particularly the receivers, as he did from himself.

Jerry Hanlon, Michigan's former offensive line coach, said the two didn't speak for nearly two months during his senior season because Harbaugh had been too harsh in his demands of the receivers.

"I told him to shut up and play quarterback," Hanlon said, in one account.

Later during that 1986 season, Harbaugh told Hanlon he finally understood, and the coach would call it a turning point in the quarterback's growth as a leader.

Jim Harbaugh's tenacity and confidence shone through in his play, as it did after scoring this touchdown against Notre Dame. Photo courtesy of Per Kjeldsen.

During his freshman year with the Wolverines, Harbaugh had led the team to a 3–1 record before breaking his left arm while diving for a loose ball against Michigan State. Harbaugh was done for the season, and the Wolverines finished with a 6–6 record.

The following year, a fully healthy Harbaugh was the nation's most efficient passer—he had a streak of 149 passes without an interception—and led Michigan to a 10–1–1 record and the Big Ten title. The Wolverines then beat Nebraska 27–23 in the Fiesta Bowl in 1986 to finish with a No. 2 national ranking.

It was in 1986 that Harbaugh also became forever entwined in Michigan–Ohio State lore. Sure, if you play in The Game, you are a part of The Game, but Harbaugh boldly stepped into the flame of the heated rivalry.

The Wolverines had won their first nine games before losing to Minnesota, and Ohio State was next. Harbaugh forcefully declared that Michigan would win the game.

"I guarantee we'll beat Ohio State and be in Pasadena New Year's Day," he told reporters.

Jamie Morris rushed for 216 yards, and Michigan backed up Harbaugh's guarantee in a 26–24 victory. Michigan next defeated Hawaii before losing in the Rose Bowl to Arizona State. The Wolverines finished 11–2, and Harbaugh was named an All-American and Big Ten Player of the Year.

57 Chad Henne: All-Time Leading Passer

It is difficult to define Chad Henne's career at Michigan.

Yes, he was a four-year starter at quarterback, the first freshman to start at the position since Rick Leach in 1975. He started 39 straight games before he suffered an injury in the second game of his senior season that kept him out of the next two games.

Yes, the kid who skipped his senior-year spring break in high school to observe the Wolverines' spring practice and study the playbook became Michigan's all-time leading passer during his career. And, yes, he guided the Wolverines to a stunning victory over Florida in the New Year's Day Capital One Bowl in 2008, his final college game.

But maybe what will define Henne's career was his stoic nature, his control of the huddle, his ability to never get rattled, and his toughness, which was there for everyone to see in his final season.

In the eighth game of the 2007 season at Illinois, Henne took a hard hit to his right throwing shoulder. He went off the field before the half, and the medical trainers tried to do something to alleviate the pain from what later was revealed to be a severe dislocation. Henne missed the third quarter but returned in the fourth to heroically spark the team to victory. He went 7-of-11 for 42 yards on two touchdown-scoring drives in the comeback victory.

After the game, his position coach, Scot Loeffler, was choked up as he talked about Henne's ability to play with a dislocated shoulder and what a courageous performance it was. The pain was so intense when Henne would take the ball from center—the impact of the snap would cause his shoulder to pop out of socket, and he would have to pop it back in—he began to work out of the shotgun.

That Henne could play with such an injury, while truly unbelievable, might not have shocked anyone who knew him. As a freshman in high school at Wilson High in West Lawn, Pennsylvania, Henne dislocated his left, non-throwing shoulder and left the game…for three plays. Trainers popped the shoulder back into socket and, two plays later, he threw a touchdown pass.

He was held out of the next game against Minnesota, but Henne would play against in-state rival Michigan State at Spartan Stadium two weeks after suffering the original injury. Clearly he was not close to 100 percent healthy, but Henne was fantastic. He threw a school-record-tying four touchdown passes, including scores of 14 and 31 yards the final two possessions of the game to erase a 10-point deficit with seven minutes left. The game-winning score was a 31-yard touchdown pass to Mario Manningham on third down with 2:28 left.

For all of Henne's ability, and with all of Michigan's offensive firepower, he completed his collegiate career without a victory over Ohio State. There's no doubt Henne wasn't healthy for that last rivalry game. He was only 11-of-34 for 68 yards in the loss.

"As hard as that game is, and as crazy as that game is, you've got to be healthy, you've got to be at your full strength to beat them," Loeffler said later. "What the kid did for four weeks, I'll never forget, and his teammates will never forget."

Henne's final game was unforgettable. Against Florida, which was led by newly crowned Heisman Trophy winner Tim Tebow, Henne was outstanding. He threw for a Michigan bowl–record 373 yards, the third-best single-game effort in school history, and had three touchdowns. Henne was named the game's MVP.

He ended his career as the all-time passing leader with 9,715 yards and 87 touchdowns, also a school record.

58 Chris Perry: The Only Doak Walker Award Winner

Perhaps Michigan should make room on its wall of All-Americans for a photograph of Irene Perry. After all, she was the main reason her son, Chris Perry, remained a Wolverine.

Chris Perry was feeling underappreciated. Anthony Thomas had become Michigan's all-time leading rusher when Perry was a freshman. The following season, Perry expected to be the No. 1 back. Instead, he was relegated to backup status on the depth chart. He finished with 495 yards and two touchdowns. Hardly the stuff of an All-American in the making.

Two seasons into his career, Perry met with coach Lloyd Carr and told him he was being underused and wasn't happy. Carr informed the young back rather firmly that he was not about to change his ways, that there is no star system at Michigan, and no one gets treated differently. Carr essentially told Perry if he couldn't deal with that, he needed to play for another team.

"When he said, 'You can transfer,' I felt he was letting me know I wasn't good enough to keep around," Perry said at the time.

Enter Irene Egerton Perry, a vibrant woman who decided to move from Advance, North Carolina, to Ann Arbor at the beginning of her son's junior year. Irene Perry had informed Carr and Perry's position coach, Fred Jackson, that she would back them if they didn't compromise her son's love for the game and his confidence.

Perry later admitted that his mother's decision to move to Michigan kept him a Wolverine.

"I had to change, had to do something to prove him wrong," Perry said. "I just wanted to prove everyone wrong."

In the Outback Bowl against Florida his junior season, Perry was named the bowl MVP after scoring four touchdowns and gaining 108 yards receiving and 85 yards rushing in the victory. Perry said that performance instilled him with confidence and was a springboard for his senior season.

During his senior season, Perry, known for his fiery enthusiasm on the field and the sideline, rushed for 1,674 yards and scored 18 touchdowns. He became the first Wolverine to win the Doak Walker Award as the nation's top running back and was named an All-American. Perry led the Big Ten in rushing, averaging 128.8

Chris Perry smiles at a news conference in Dallas in February 2004, where he was introduced as the 2003 Doak Walker Award recipient. The award was created in 1989 to recognize the premier collegiate running back for his accomplishments on the field, achievement in the classroom, and citizenship in the community.

yards, was named the conference's Player of the Year, and finished fourth in Heisman Trophy voting.

Perhaps his most impressive moment was at Michigan State when he set a single-game Michigan record with 51 carries—nine more than the previous record shared by Ron Johnson and Anthony Thomas—in a 27–20 victory. He rushed for 219 yards against the Spartans.

"I was never aware of breaking a record," Perry said. "I just wanted to win."

After that performance against the Spartans, Carr summed up Perry and his journey as a Wolverine.

"Perry has the heart of a champion," Carr said. "I love that kid and the way he's played and the career he's had at Michigan."

59 Tom Brady: A Tale of Competition and Confidence

Quarterback Tom Brady started the final 25 games of his Michigan career and was 20–5 as the starter, but his career was not nearly as drama-free as those statistics might suggest. Brady, who went on to stardom in the NFL with the New England Patriots, was considering transferring from the Wolverines in 1996 as a freshman and visited coach Lloyd Carr to inform him he didn't feel he was being treated fairly in a quarterback competition with Brian Griese and Scott Dreisbach.

"I said, 'Coach, you're not giving me a fair shake. I'm the best quarterback you have,'" Brady recalled later. "He said, 'Why don't you quit worrying about yourself? Quit worrying about the weather. Quit worrying about the bad calls. Go out and do the best you can do.'"

Carr also remembered the meeting.

"Tom was adamant at that point that he was the best quarterback," Carr said. "Brady has never been a guy who lacked confidence, which is good."

Brady didn't quit, but the challenges didn't end there. In 1998, when it appeared he would have the job locked up, in came freshman phenom Drew Henson. Brady earned the starting job, but they shared playing time throughout the season. Several years later, Brady, who started every game in 1998 and 1999, admitted the competition with Henson was mentally grueling.

"He came in and he was a great athlete and he could really play quarterback," Brady said. "It was competition every day. I swear to God, it was almost tougher on the practice field than it was on the game field. You always put so much pressure on yourself.

Tom Brady passes in the second quarter against Penn State in November 1998. Brady completed 17 of 30 passes for 224 yards and two touchdowns to beat Penn State 27–0.

"I think that competition is really what served me well as the years have gone on, just the ability to worry about yourself and focus on what you can do to get better. Looking back, that was the turning point in my football career."

Brady, voted a tri-captain his senior year, helped lead the Wolverines to a share of the Big Ten title in 1998 and was named the team's Most Valuable Player. He led the team to victory in the 1999 Citrus Bowl, and in the Orange Bowl on New Year's Day 2000, Brady was at his best. He led the Wolverines back from a pair of 14-point deficits to beat Alabama 35–34 in overtime and played brilliantly. He was 34-of-46 for 369 yards and a career-best four touchdowns. Brady became known as the "Comeback Kid" for his late-game heroics during the 1999 season.

During his career, Brady completed 63 percent of his passes for 5,351 yards, 35 touchdowns, and 19 interceptions. He threw for

2,586 yards and had 20 touchdowns and six interceptions during his senior year.

While Brady earned national praise for his leadership, toughness, and poise, his NFL stock was not all that high. He had a slow time in the 40-yard dash at the combine, but in the days before the draft, Brady was clear about what kind of athlete he had become while at Michigan.

"I'm the type of player, the type of team player, that any team would look for," Brady said. "I think the ability is there. In terms of all the physical skills, I can do whatever it takes."

Brady was drafted in the sixth round by the New England Patriots and has since led the Patriots to five Super Bowl appearances and three Super Bowl championships, earning the Super Bowl MVP award twice.

60 Gary Moeller: The Man Who Followed a Legend

As fond as Bo Schembechler was of running the ball whenever possible, his successor, Gary Moeller, was just as fond of the forward pass.

Imagine that, a Michigan coach who liked to throw. "I know you guys are going to like him," Bo said to the gathered media when Moeller was formally introduced as the new head coach. "You'll see more passing, I guarantee you that. He knows that side of the game and likes to pass. But if he doesn't run the ball, he'd be a damned fool."

Schembechler said that? Really?

Both coaches laughed, of course.

Moeller was on Schembechler's staff at Miami (Ohio) for the 1967 and 1968 seasons and moved with him to Michigan in 1969. He was the defensive ends coach until 1973, when Moeller was promoted to defensive coordinator. His defenses in 1974, 1976, and 1985 led the nation in scoring defense.

He left Michigan to become Illinois head coach in 1977, but that didn't last long. After three losing seasons, he was fired.

"I learned a lot that will help me from that job," Moeller said of Illinois. "I learned that you can't do it all yourself and that you must have support from the top."

Moeller returned to Schembechler's staff in 1980 as the quarterbacks coach, then resumed coordinating the defense from 1982 to 1987. He tried his hand at coordinating the offense for three seasons beginning in 1987, and then he became head coach. As with anyone succeeding a legend, Moeller knew he had enormous shoes to fill.

"I know it will be hard replacing Bo," Moeller said at the time. "This will be Gary Moeller's program, but it will have a lot of Bo Schembechler in it."

After taking over for Schembechler in 1990, Moeller guided the Wolverines to four bowl victories in five years, including the 1993 Rose Bowl victory over Washington. His teams won three Big Ten championships, including two outright, went to five straight bowls, and finished in the nation's top 20 five straight seasons.

Moeller, like Schembechler, had a deep Ohio State connection. He was a three-year letter winner, playing center and linebacker for OSU and was a cocaptain as a senior. It was there he became acquainted with Schembechler, an assistant under Woody Hayes. Moeller began his coaching career after graduating from OSU in 1963.

Although he trained under Schembechler and absorbed similar ways of approaching football, Moeller's coaching demeanor was much different. Like Schembechler, Moeller was a fiend when it came to watching film and breaking it down, and like Schembechler, practices were a favorite time during the season because of the work, the teaching, and the camaraderie. But unlike Schembechler, who had a more gruff approach with the players, Moeller was calmer and wasn't one to raise his voice much. While Moeller was serious about his devotion to football, he loved to have fun with his players, and he never projected a sense of ego.

The Michigan players liked the fact that Moeller would maintain the Michigan tradition but offer a new twist in terms of a more open offense. Still, Moeller never disagreed with his boss that running the ball and playing tough defense were the keys to victory.

"Obviously, I'm not Bo," Moeller said at the time. "I can't tell you what I am. I'd rather show the people with hard work. It's funny, but when he got mad, Bo would always tell me, 'Wait until you have this damned job someday.'"

During his five seasons as Michigan head coach, Moeller was 44–13–3 for a winning percentage of .758. The Wolverines won 78 percent of their Big Ten games, as well. Moeller's career at Michigan ended suddenly when he resigned in April 1995 after he was arrested on a charge of disorderly conduct at a metro-Detroit restaurant. He was succeeded by Lloyd Carr, who had been an assistant under Moeller at Illinois and worked with him on Michigan's staff.

61 Wolverines Going Bowling...

You never forget your first. Michigan played in the first Rose Bowl on January 1, 1902, and handily defeated Stanford 49–0. Thus began a long relationship between the Wolverines and the New Year's Day bowl game known nationally as the "Granddaddy of Them All."

"It's the greatest tradition in college football," former Michigan coach Lloyd Carr once said of the Rose Bowl. "I've always felt that there's no better experience for a college football player than to play in the Rose Bowl."

Michigan's Bowl Record

Note: From 1918 to 1945, the Big Ten did not allow its teams to participate in bowls. From 1946 to 1974, only the conference champion was allowed to attend a bowl (the Rose Bowl), and no team could go in consecutive years (one exception was Ohio State in 1972 and 1973).

Year	Bowl	Result
2011	Sugar	Michigan 23, Virginia Tech 20
2010	Gator	Mississippi State 52, Michigan 14
2008	Capital One	Michigan 41, Florida 35
2007	Rose	USC 32, Michigan 18
2005	Alamo	Nebraska 32, Michigan 28
2004	Rose	Texas 38, Michigan 37
2003	Rose	USC 28, Michigan 14
2002	Outback	Michigan 38, Florida 30
2001	Citrus	Tennessee 45, Michigan 17
2000	Citrus	Michigan 31, Auburn 28
1999	Orange	Michigan 35, Alabama 34 (OT)
1998	Citrus	Michigan 45, Arkansas 31
1997	Rose	Michigan 21, Washington State 16
1996	Outback	Alabama 17, Michigan 14
1995	Alamo	Texas A&M 22, Michigan 20
1994	Holiday	Michigan 24, Colorado State 14
1993	Hall of Fame	Michigan 42, North Carolina State 7
1992	Rose	Michigan 38, Washington 31
1991	Rose	Washington 34, Michigan 14
1990	Gator	Michigan 35, Mississippi 3
1989	Rose	USC 17, Michigan 10
1988	Rose	Michigan 22, USC 14
1987	Hall of Fame	Michigan 28, Alabama 24
1986	Rose	Arizona State 22, Michigan 15
1985	Fiesta	Michigan 27, Nebraska 23
1984	Holiday	Brigham Young 24, Michigan 17
1983	Sugar	Auburn 9, Michigan 7
1982	Rose	UCLA 24, Michigan 14
1981	Bluebonnet	Michigan 33, UCLA 14
1980	Rose	Michigan 23, Washington 6
1979	Gator	North Carolina 17, Michigan 15
1978	Rose	USC 17, Michigan 10
1977	Rose	Washington 27, Michigan 20
1976	Rose	USC 14, Michigan 6
1975	Orange	Oklahoma 14, Michigan 6
1971	Rose	Stanford 13, Michigan 12
1969	Rose	USC 10, Michigan 3
1964	Rose	Michigan 34, Oregon State 7
1950	Rose	Michigan 14, California 6
1948	Rose	Michigan 49, Southern Cal 0
1902	Rose	Michigan 49, Stanford 0

The Rose Bowl is one of the loveliest settings in all of sports. The stadium is in Pasadena in Southern California, and was built in the gorge called the Arroyo Seco. The San Gabriel Mountains are to the north.

Until 2009, Michigan had played in 33 straight bowl games and 39 overall. The Wolverines have been to the Rose Bowl 20 times, although not with great success, considering their 8–12 record. Still, the Rose Bowl has held great memories for Michigan, as well. In the 1948 game under coach Fritz Crisler, the Wolverines entered ranked No. 2 and walloped USC 49–0. Voters, in an unprecedented move, held another vote after that game, giving Michigan the national championship. Notre Dame had been voted the pre-bowl national championship.

On New Year's Day in 1998 the Wolverines maintained their perfect season by beating Washington State 21–16, and earned a share of the national championship under Carr's watch.

Michigan's streak of 33 straight bowl games ended in 2008 when the Wolverines endured their first losing season since 1967. They returned to the postseason in the 2011 Gator Bowl but suffered the program's worst defeat, 52–14, to Mississippi State under Rich Rodriguez. Just more than year later, coached by Brady Hoke, the Wolverines capped a 10–2 regular season with a BCS Sugar Bowl victory over Virginia Tech.

62 Dennis Franklin: Michigan Quarterback

Dennis Franklin worked hard throughout his Michigan career that began in 1972 to simply be a Michigan quarterback. There are no other qualifiers than that. He wanted to be "Dennis Franklin, Michigan quarterback."

But every time he would do an interview and every time he was written about, it was always, "Dennis Franklin, Michigan's first black quarterback."

"It became annoying," Franklin said not long ago in his home-town newspaper, the *Canton Repository*. "Eventually, it went away. That's all I ever strived for."

Franklin became the starter as a sophomore in 1972, winning the job from Tom Slade, who the previous season had led Michigan to an 11–1 record, its only loss a 13–12 decision against Stanford in the Rose Bowl. During his first season, Franklin led Michigan to a 10–1 record, its only loss at Ohio State 14–11.

"'The Menace' has been developing beyond anything we could have hoped," Michigan coach Bo Schembechler said at the time of his young starter. "He's getting smoother and better and smarter every day."

During his career, Franklin led the Wolverines to a 30–2–1 record as a starter, and they won three consecutive Big Ten titles from 1972 to 1974, but, sadly, Michigan would never go to a bowl game with Franklin leading the offense.

He was at the center of it all—and not because he wanted to be—in 1973 during the big Michigan–Ohio State Big Ten Rose Bowl controversy. Michigan and Ohio State met at Michigan Stadium on November 24, the Buckeyes ranked No. 1 and the Wolverines No. 4.

The teams struggled mightily. The Buckeyes led 10–0 at half-time, but Michigan came back and tied the game on Franklin's 10-yard run midway through the fourth quarter. Late in the game, the Wolverines were clicking offensively and had moved to mid-field. With just more than two minutes remaining, Franklin was hit hard as he released a pass and landed on his right shoulder. His collarbone was broken.

Michigan missed a field goal when it had a chance to win the game, and it ended at 10–10.

Because of the no-repeat rule, Michigan should have gone to the Rose Bowl. But the Big Ten athletics directors were polled by the league the next day. Michigan athletics director Don Canham was confident his colleagues would vote for the Wolverines and even predicted to reporters that it would be a 9–1 vote in their favor.

Actually it was a 6–4 vote, and Ohio State won the right to represent the conference in the Rose Bowl. Most believe the six athletics directors who voted against Michigan did so because of Franklin's injury and because they thought the Wolverines would not have a chance to win without him.

The Wolverines would stay home for the holidays, and Michigan coach Bo Schembechler was angry. Franklin would later say he was devastated by the news. Schembechler returned to Ann Arbor from Detroit, where he had been told of the vote, and didn't know how to explain it to his players.

Franklin was voted a team captain in 1974 and was a first-team All–Big Ten quarterback after that season. He led the team in passing and total offense during his three years, at that time becoming only the second player in program history since Tom Harmon to accomplish that feat for three consecutive seasons.

Michigan went 10–1 in 1974, its only loss to Ohio State, and Franklin would go on to finish sixth in Heisman Trophy balloting.

63 Reggie McKenzie: Standout Lineman

Offensive linemen get their due…sometimes.

While the hardworking tailback, the flashy receiver, and the quarterback grab the headlines and provide the television and radio sound bites after games, the offensive lineman are generally acknowledged but not overly acclaimed.

But at Michigan, there have been quite a few linemen who have stood out over the years, and one of them was Reggie McKenzie, a consensus All-American in 1971.

McKenzie, whose Michigan playing career began in 1969, was a linemate of Dan Dierdorf for two seasons, and they helped produce one of the more formidable lines in program history. McKenzie was praised as one of the nation's top pulling guards, and he twice was named first-team All–Big Ten.

During his three seasons, Michigan saw nearly all of the program's rushing records broken. McKenzie played on two Big Ten champions and two Rose Bowl teams.

"He was a great, great player," former coach Bo Schembechler once said. "He was one of the truly great guards who could pull and then run with any back we had. He came in as an unheralded player and then worked to become one of the great players on our team. What makes me even more proud of Reggie is what he did after his football career was over and how he developed his foundation."

McKenzie was still playing in the NFL, a star lineman with the Buffalo Bills after being drafted in the second round, when he decided to give back. He played 13 seasons in the NFL, including 11 with the Bills.

For McKenzie, there was a much bigger world beyond the NFL, but he knew through football and sports he could make a difference. He decided in 1974 to create the Reggie McKenzie Foundation, which focuses its efforts on Detroit youth. The foundation addresses their needs through sports, health awareness, and academics.

He started a football camp in his hometown of Highland Park in Detroit and ran that three-day camp with 50 kids in 1974 on a tight budget. Often, McKenzie would head back to his old stomping grounds of Ann Arbor and borrow football equipment, mostly footballs and cones, from Schembechler.

Now, the Foundation runs five sports camps and four academic programs, still on a shoestring budget of about $500,000 annually, mostly from donations, sponsorships, grants, and volunteers. It serves more than 1,500 students and doesn't charge them a dime.

The free football, basketball, tennis, and track programs run throughout the year. There's also a golf camp.

McKenzie has made a point throughout the years to offer instruction. Among his students were Pepper Johnson, who went on to play in the NFL and later work for the foundation, and Jerome Bettis, a Super Bowl champion with the Pittsburgh Steelers.

Still, while so much of the foundation revolves around athletics, academics are absolutely the focus for McKenzie. The foundation offers standardized test preparation and a drug- awareness program, and the ultimate overall goal of the instruction is to promote self-esteem and self-confidence.

McKenzie's football career still is in the forefront, though. In 2002 he was inducted into the College Football Hall of Fame as part of a 13-player, two-coach class.

"Being called an All-American at the University of Michigan and being selected to the College Football Hall of Fame are huge," McKenzie said at the time. "I truly feel blessed and greatly honored.

"I often thought it would be nice [to be inducted], but I didn't know the criteria. It's an honor. I enjoyed playing the game of football. Number one, to be able to go to the University of Michigan, and number two, to be selected to the College Football Hall of Fame—those are big deals."

64 Braylon Edwards: Unstoppable Receiver

When Braylon Edwards arrived at Michigan, he was a young, talented, physically gifted Detroit native with the brash, fun attitude, the wild hair, and the dad who played football at Michigan.

When Braylon Edwards left Michigan after the conclusion of his senior year in 2004, he was a seasoned athlete, more mature, even more skilled than when he arrived, and coveted by NFL teams. Oh, and his hair was shorter and more, well, professional.

Edwards was a star at Michigan in every way. He looked like one. He talked like one. And he played like one.

The 6'3", 208-pounder had 1,330 receiving yards his senior season to become the first player in Big Ten history and ninth in Division I-A football history to surpass the 1,000-yard mark three times during his career. During his senior season, Edwards set Michigan season records for receptions (97) and yards (1,330), and he also became the Wolverines' all-time career leader in receiving yards with 3,541, passing Anthony Carter's mark and setting the record for career catches (252) and touchdowns (39).

Michigan coach Lloyd Carr would call Edwards "a threat" every time he touched the ball. Like most Michigan receivers, Edwards became an excellent blocking receiver who prided himself on that ability, calling it "the dirty work" that allowed other players to do their things to gain positive yardage.

But mainly, he was a breathtaking receiver who was ridiculously difficult to cover in man coverage, as many cornerbacks discovered.

"In man and one-on-one coverage, I don't think anybody could stop me," Edwards said at the time.

Braylon Edwards makes a touchdown catch in the back of the end zone against Miami (Ohio) in September 2004. Edwards caught 97 passes for 1,330 yards and 15 touchdowns in 2004.

He won the Fred Biletnikoff Award, which goes to the nation's best receiver, after his fine senior season. Edwards also was the Big Ten MVP and was named an All-American.

That final season almost didn't materialize. Edwards, who was in and out of Carr's doghouse early in his career because he was late to a team meeting, had considered leaving early for the NFL. Ultimately, he decided he needed to finish his college career.

"Getting a chance to wear that winged helmet for another season," Edwards said, "allowed me to mature as a man and allowed me to leave the nest and go out in the real world."

At the beginning of his Michigan career, he wore jersey No. 80, but before his junior year, he was allowed to take the No. 1 jersey that Carter had worn with such success. Edwards has since endowed a scholarship at Michigan for any player who wears that number.

While he may never be forgotten for his phenomenal performance in Michigan's 45–37 triple-overtime victory over Michigan State at Michigan Stadium, a game that he almost single-handedly turned, Edwards also was a bright spot in the Wolverines' 38–37 loss to Texas in the Rose Bowl.

He ended his Michigan career—wearing No. 1, of course—with three touchdown receptions, tying a bowl record, and 109 yards. Edwards was Edwards, and did it all well that game, whether it meant outleaping everyone else in the end zone for a touchdown or taking the quick pass to gain a first down. His first touchdown in that Rose Bowl was a deep strike from freshman quarterback Chad Henne. Edwards was in double coverage, and his focus was so intense, he managed to maintain ball and body control before falling out of bounds.

"He was a great football player on the field, he was a great leader on our team, and the thing that I'm very, very proud of—and that I had nothing to do with—he was a great person off the field," Carr said. "He's been a great representative of the University of Michigan, and that goes back to the day he came here."

65 The Game 2003: No. 100

Michigan–Ohio State never gets old. The two teams played the 100th game of their series on November 22, 2003, at Michigan Stadium, and even after that one ended, everyone was ready for the next meeting—and the one after that, and the one after that, and so on.

The teams first played in 1897—anyone remember?—with Michigan winning 34–0.

In 2003, as usual, there was plenty on the line as No. 4 Ohio State ventured to Ann Arbor to face No. 5 Michigan before an NCAA-record 112,118 at Michigan Stadium. The Big Ten title was up for grabs, and Ohio State was still hoping for a shot at the national championship game.

Michigan senior tailback Chris Perry, a Heisman Trophy finalist and eventual Doak Walker Award winner, rushed for 154 yards and two touchdowns to lead the Wolverines to a 35–21 victory. Receiver Braylon Edwards had seven catches for 130 yards and two touchdowns.

The Wolverines won their 41st Big Ten title and clinched a Rose Bowl berth, while Ohio State dropped out of the Sugar Bowl race and its thoughts of repeating as national champions were squelched. Both teams finished the regular season with 10–2 records.

"You are in the eye of the storm," Michigan coach Lloyd Carr said after the game, referring to the emotions at play each and every time Michigan and Ohio State face each other. "You know you're going to be as disappointed as you can be in losing, and you know the euphoria you will experience if you win."

Thanks to Perry's 30-yard touchdown run, Michigan took a 28–7 third-quarter lead. But the Buckeyes wouldn't go away. They cut the deficit to 28–21 on Lydell Ross' two-yard touchdown run early in the fourth quarter. The Buckeyes who had made a habit of winning games by small margins—they had won 12 games the last two years by seven points or fewer—looked like they were staging an unlikely comeback.

Michigan's offense flinched late in the game when John Navarre's pass intended for Edwards was intercepted by Chris Gamble. The Buckeyes got the ball on their own 37-yard line, but Michigan's defense forced a three-and-out.

"That was the turning point, going three-and-out after the interception," Krenzel said.

Steve Breaston, Michigan's receiver and kick returner, then fumbled a punt near the Michigan end zone, but Leon Hall jumped on the loose ball. The Wolverines drove 88 yards in eight plays, and Perry scored on a 15-yard run with just under eight minutes left to take a two-touchdown lead.

Perry, who battled a leg injury during the game, averaged five yards a carry against an Ohio State defense that had been yielding an average 55 yards rushing per game.

"I had some problems," he would say later, "but I was not going to come out."

As for Navarre, much-maligned throughout his Michigan career, winning the Big Ten trophy in his final regular-season game by beating Ohio State was more than rewarding. He choked back tears after the game, but during, he was steady, completing 21 of 32 passes for 278 yards and two touchdowns.

This had been a challenging season for Navarre and the Wolverines, who started the season with a 4–2 record and never looked to be in the race for the Big Ten championship. But they staged a monumental turnaround with a 38–35 comeback victory at Minnesota, scoring 31 points in the fourth quarter. That sparked a six-game winning streak, including the win over Ohio State in the 100th game.

"The test of leadership always comes when things go poorly," Carr said. "These guys stood the test."

66 Big Ten Road Trips: A Guide for UM Fans in Columbus

There are the rare Michigan fans, not including parents of players, of course, who don't miss a game, home or away.

But for those—the greater majority—who don't have the time to devote 12 weekends every fall to the Wolverines, but would like to add, say, one road trip a season, there are some terrific destinations in the Big Ten.

For starters, there are three must-do trips, although all 10 college towns are worth visiting. Not in any particular order, the recommended trips are to Wisconsin (in Madison), Penn State (in State College), and, if you're brave enough, Ohio State (in Columbus).

The game-day experience at the University of Wisconsin in Madison is unbeatable, and there's plenty to do in town before and after. The crowd at a Wisconsin game is an eclectic mix, and overall, it can be a rowdy, fun group. Beer and brats pretty much comprise the pregame menu, even if kickoff is at noon.

Night starts are the most enjoyable at Camp Randall Stadium, since fans have had a day to enjoy the buildup to the game. Besides watching Bucky the Badger, Wisconsin's mascot, cruise the sideline, one in-game tradition that you need to be in your seat for—actually, you'll be out of your seat—occurs between the third and fourth quarters. The crowd completely lets go as House of Pain's "Jump Around" is played. It is three minutes of total zaniness.

Stick around after the game in the stadium for the 5th Quarter. This is one of the most recognizable traditions of the Wisconsin marching band, as it marches onto the field, faces the winning team's stands, and plays that team's school song. Then they turn to the other side and play the song of the losing team. Then the band performs a number of songs, like "Beer Barrel Polka" and "Tequila." At the end of the 15-minute bonus performance, the band once more plays "Varsity."

Don't miss visiting Madison or the campus. Stop in at the Wisconsin student union and eat at Der Rathskeller, which has been around for three-quarters of a century and features an all-day menu and often has live music.

Getting to Penn State is the biggest challenge for Michigan fans. There are only two daily direct flights from Detroit, and the drive is a bit of a haul, but once you get to Happy Valley, you'll find it's worth it. This is a true college town, and the campus has a distinct eastern feel. There are old-style taverns that typically have long lines the night before a football game. Make sure to visit the All-American Rathskeller to take in the atmosphere and to shoot pool. There are plenty of diners and shops, and a trip to Penn State would not be complete without a stop at the Creamery to have "Peachy Paterno" ice cream.

Game days are all about the tailgate in State College, as fans and their cars pack in, side by side, in the grassy lots surrounding Beaver Stadium. They are friendly fans who have never seemed to mind mingling with their guests wearing maize and blue, pre- and postgame.

As a Michigan fan, a trip to Ohio State should be on the schedule, if only once during a lifetime. It is, after all, The Game, and seeing it in the Horseshoe certainly is a memorable, unforgettable experience.

Those Wolverines fans who have made the trip to Columbus offer helpful tips. Many have said that cars with Michigan license plates are targeted by area police, so driving *under* the speed limit is recommended.

Before the game in 2006 that featured No. 1 Ohio State facing No. 2 Michigan, an email offering safety tips for traveling to Columbus was sent to UM students and alumni. "Keep your Michigan gear to a minimum, or wait until you are inside the stadium to display it," the email, signed by the Alumni Association and dean of students, indicated. Also, "If verbally harassed by opposing fans, don't take the bait."

There is plenty to do in Columbus before and after a game, though. If heading into the city isn't part of the plan and sticking around campus is, High Street is a popular area with a variety of eating and drinking establishments. The Buckeye Hall of Fame café offers a nostalgic look at the Ohio State program. Make sure to stop at the Varsity Club, established in 1959 and located about 500 yards from the stadium.

If you really want to get into the spirit of the game, two hours before each Ohio State home football game, the Ohio State marching band performs in the "Skull Session." The Skull Session, which has its roots in the early 1930s, is a wildly popular concert/pep rally at St. John Arena. Often, the visiting school's marching band performs, as well.

As for the other Big Ten road trips, Iowa is another fun stop. Definitely visit the Pedestrian Mall and the Hamburg Inn, the best of the greasy spoon restaurants in Iowa City. Illinois has one of the most cheerful tailgate settings in the Big Ten, and then there's Minnesota, with its big-city attractions. The Gophers' new stadium is expected to return the "college-feel." Northwestern is a fun trip because, if you're traveling from southeast Michigan, taking the train to Chicago makes for a throwback weekend. There's plenty to do in the city and in Evanston. Make sure to get a hot dog from Mustard's Last Stand, located across from Ryan Field.

Going to a game at Michigan State is a no-brainer—the campus is one of the prettiest around, and the football can be some of the nastiest. If visiting all the Big Ten stadiums is your goal, so be it, but don't rush to schedule trips to Purdue or Indiana.

67 Michigan's Major Trophy/ Award Winners

For a football program that has never, ever made a habit of campaigning for postseason awards—nope, Michigan has never sent gimmicky magnets or weekly postcards to garner votes, nor has there ever been, or ever will be, a Michigan player prominently displayed on the side of a building in Times Square—Michigan has earned its share of major awards and trophies.

The Heisman Trophy has been awarded since 1935 by the Downtown Athletic Club of New York, and Michigan has had three winners. Tom Harmon won in 1940, Desmond Howard in 1991, and Charles Woodson, who became the first primarily defensive player to win, received the honor in 1997.

Excluding those three, Michigan has had 17 players earn votes for the Heisman. Bob Chappuis in 1947 finished second, and more recently, tailback Mike Hart finished fifth in 2006 and quarterback Denard Robinson finished sixth in 2010.

What's it like to earn college football's famous piece of hardware?

When Woodson heard his name called, he dropped to one knee at the foot of the podium at the Downtown Athletic Club, prayed, hugged his mother, Georgia, and then embraced the Heisman Trophy.

"My body just went limp," Woodson said. "I just had to grasp what had really happened."

In 2004 Braylon Edwards, Michigan's talented, prolific receiver became the program's first and only winner of the Fred Biletnikoff

Michigan Players and the Heisman Trophy

Year	Player	Place
1939	Tom Harmon	2
1940	Tom Harmon	Winner
1941	Bob Westfall	8
1943	Bill Daley	7
1947	Bob Chappuis	2
1955	Ron Kramer	8
1956	Ron Kramer	6
1964	Bob Timberlake	4
1968	Ron Johnson	6
1974	Dennis Franklin	6
1975	Gordon Bell	8
1976	Rob Lytle	3
1977	Rick Leach	8
1978	Rick Leach	3
1980	Anthony Carter	10
1981	Anthony Carter	7
1982	Anthony Carter	4
1986	Jim Harbaugh	3
1991	Desmond Howard	Winner
1993	Tyrone Wheatley	8
1994	Tyrone Wheatley	12
1995	Tshimanga Biakabutuka	8
1997	Charles Woodson	Winner
2003	Chris Perry	4
2004	Braylon Edwards	10
2006	Mike Hart	5
2010	Denard Robinson	6

Award, which was first presented in 1994 to the nation's top receiver. In 2003 tailback Chris Perry became Michigan's first and only Doak Walker Award winner as the nation's top running back among juniors and seniors.

David Baas in 2004 was co-winner of the Rimington Trophy as the nation's outstanding center, but he wasn't the last—David Molk, a tri-captain, won the award in 2011.

Making It to the Hall

The College Football Hall of Fame located in South Bend, Indiana, is not reserved solely for players. Five Michigan coaches are among those in the Hall.

Player	Years at UM	Position	Induction
Albert Benbrook	1908–1910	Guard	1971
David Brown	1972–1974	Defensive back	2007
Anthony Carter	1979–1982	Wide receiver	2001
Bob Chappuis	1942, 1946–1947	Halfback	1988
Tom Curtis	1967–1969	Defensive back	2005
Dan Dierdorf	1968–1970	Tackle	2000
Bump Elliott	1946–1947	Halfback	1989
Pete Elliott	1945–1948	Quarterback	1994
Benny Friedman	1924–1926	Quarterback	1951
Tom Harmon	1938–1940	Halfback	1954
Willie Heston	1901–1904	Halfback	1954
Elroy Hirsch	1943	Halfback	1974
Desmond Howard	1989–1991	Wide receiver	2010
Ron Johnson	1966–1968	Halfback	1992
Harry Kipke	1921–1923	Halfback	1958
Ron Kramer	1954–1956	End	1978
Jim Mandich	1967–1969	End	2005
John Maulbetsch	1914–1916	Halfback	1973
Reggie McKenzie	1969–1971	Guard	2002
William Morley	1895	Halfback	1971
Harry Newman	1930–1932	Quarterback	1975
Bennie Oosterbaan	1925–1927	End	1954
Merv Pregulman	1941–1943	Guard/Tackle	1982
Adolph Schulz	1904–1908	Center	1951
Neil Snow	1898–1901	End/Fullback	1960
Ernie Vick	1918–1921	Center	1983
Bob Westfall	1939–1941	Fullback	1987
Albert Wistert	1940–1942	Tackle	1968
Alvin Wistert	1946–1949	Tackle	1981
Francis Wistert	1931–1933	Tackle	1967
Lloyd Carr	1995–2007	Coach	2011
Fritz Crisler	1938–1947	Coach	1954
George Little	1922–1924	Coach	1955
Bo Schembechler	1969–1989	Coach	1993
Tad Wieman	1921–1928	Coach	1956
Fielding Yost	1901–1923, 1925–1926	Coach	1951

Four Michigan coaches have won the AFCA Coach of the Year Award: Fritz Crisler in 1947, Bennie Oosterbaan in 1948 (Michigan is the only school to have back-to-back winners), Bo Schembechler in 1969, and Lloyd Carr in 1997.

Jim Herrmann was the Broyles Award winner in 1997 as the nation's top assistant coach. He was defensive coordinator of the national title team. Fred Jackson was AFCA assistant coach of the year in 2001.

Erick Anderson in 1991 became the only Michigan player to win the Butkus Award, given to the nation's top linebacker, and in 2006, defensive lineman LaMarr Woodley became the first Wolverine to win the Lombardi Award, given to the outstanding lineman of the year.

In 2004 Braylon Edwards, Michigan's talented, prolific receiver became the program's first and only winner of the Fred Biletnikoff Award, which was first presented in 1994 to the nation's top receiver. In 2003 tailback Chris Perry became Michigan's first and only Doak Walker Award winner as the nation's top running back among juniors and seniors.

Finally, Michigan's David Baas in 2004 was a co-winner of the Dave Rimington Trophy as the nation's outstanding center.

Four Michigan coaches have won the AFCA Coach of the Year Award—Fritz Crisler in 1947, Bennie Oosterbaan in 1948, Bo Schembechler in 1969, and Lloyd Carr in 1997. Michigan is the only school to have back-to-back winners, Crisler and Oosterbaan.

Former defensive coordinator Jim Herrmann was the Broyles Award winner in 1997 as the nation's top assistant coach. Fred Jackson won the AFCA assistant coach of the year in 2001.

68 Michigan-MSU 2003

The 2003 game at Michigan State was as much about Michigan winning 27–20 on a gray, rainy day, as it was about Chris Perry.

It was an individual performance that would have made Bo Schembechler proud.

Perry, the Wolverines' top tailback, entered that game on November 1 as the Big Ten's leading rusher, averaging 121.6 yards a game. He had a Michigan single-game record 51 carries for 219 yards. He smashed the previous record of 42 that had been shared by Ron Johnson (Northwestern, 1967) and Anthony Thomas (Indiana, 1999). Perry had one rushing touchdown in the victory.

He later said he had no idea he was closing in on the record, although he knew he had 25 carries at halftime.

"[Running backs] Coach [Fred] Jackson kept telling me I'm always running my mouth that I can carry the ball a lot of times, and he said, 'You're going to get your chance,'" Perry said. "I didn't think he was serious, though."

Michigan pounded Michigan State for 219 yards rushing and 29 first downs. Michigan State mustered just 36 yards and 13 first downs. As has been the case more often than not in the Michigan–Michigan State rivalry, the team that gains the most yards rushing typically wins the game. With this performance, that made it 33 of the last 34 games in the rivalry to be decided by the rushing totals.

Not unexpectedly, the Wolverines dominated in time of possession with 39 minutes, 38 seconds, thanks mostly to Perry, the difference-maker. But Perry needed strong offensive line play and he got it.

"The offensive line was awesome," Michigan quarterback John Navarre said after the game. "And Chris ran well."

Understatement of that season.

Navarre also played well. Before the game, MSU defensive end Greg Taplin said he believed the Spartans were the better team and he also called Navarre a "sitting duck." Taplin predicted the defensive front would smother Navarre and never give him a chance to run the offense.

The key word there, of course, was "run." That's where Perry came in. Michigan coach Lloyd Carr heaped praise on his star back after the game.

"He's not a flashy guy, but what an unbelievable football player he is," Carr said. "He can catch the football. When we get into games where we have to throw the football and where we want to throw the football, he's a devastating pass blocker. He can run with power, and he can run outside, too. Perry is a great back."

For Michigan players, beating Michigan State is about bragging rights, just as it is for Michigan State when the Spartans beat the Wolverines.

But all the bragging after this victory was about Perry and his 51 carries. "He just gave everything he had," said receiver Braylon Edwards. "He never got tired, he never asked to come off the field."

Early in the fourth quarter, Perry took a helmet to his right thigh, already sore from the Purdue game a week earlier. He never asked to come out of the game.

"He just kept going," said guard David Baas. "You can always tell when you look in a player's eyes. The whole team wanted it bad."

Perry said removing himself from the game was never an option. The only option was winning it.

"I was never aware of any records," he said. "I just wanted to get the win."

69 Garrett Rivas and Remy Hamilton: Memorable Kickers

Everyone knows the whole thing about kickers—they aren't really football players and they aren't really noticed until they miss a critical kick or until they kick a game winner that becomes etched in the memories of all who watched.

If kickers go out and do their jobs, everyone is happy.

Garrett Rivas, a 5'9", 216-pound kicker, found that out during his Michigan career (2003 to 2006), as did Remy Hamilton (1993 to 1996).

By the end of his career, Rivas was the Wolverines' all-time leading scorer with 354 points and also its career leader in most point-after-touchdowns scored with 162. He also had the most field goals scored in a career with 64.

Hamilton scored 63 field goals and has the Michigan single-season record with 25. Rivas and Hamilton tied for most career field goals attempted with 82.

Both accounted for some of the more memorable field goals in recent Michigan history.

Rivas kicked a 35-yarder in overtime to lift the Wolverines over Michigan State 34–31 in 2005, and he also kicked a 33-yard field goal with 47 seconds left at Minnesota to cap Michigan's 31-point fourth quarter in the 38–35 comeback victory in 2003. That's pretty memorable for a guy who liked the fact that he looked more like a football player than most kickers and toughed out so many kicks to give Michigan an edge.

"When you think of a kicker, you think of a really scrawny guy who never hangs out with anybody," Rivas said during his career. "I don't associate myself with a typical kicker. I'm just a football player. That's about it."

Memorable Michigan Field Goals

Date	Qtr./Time Opponent	Yards	Kicker	Result
10-1-2005	OT at Michigan State	35	Garrett Rivas	Michigan 34–31
10-10-2003	4th/:47 at Minnesota	33	Rivas	Michigan 38–35
8-31-2002	4th/:00 Washington	44	Philip Brabbs	Michigan 31–29
9-10-1994	4th/:00 at Notre Dame	42	Remy Hamilton	Michigan 26–24
11-24-1990	4th/:00 at Ohio State	37	J.D. Carlson	Michigan 16–13
9-23-1989	4th/:01 at UCLA	24	Carlson	Michigan 24–23

He considered himself so much like everyone else that Rivas went through the same weightlifting program as the rest of the team. What Rivas knew is that because he was on the shorter side, he needed to utilize a more compact swing—his momentum came from his overall strength.

Hamilton, a soccer-style kicker, also provided a big kick for the Michigan scrapbook. He became a national star in 1994 when he made the game-winning 42-yard field goal with no time left to beat Notre Dame in his first career start.

"I came in and hit the game winner, and what was going through my mind after that game was, 'Now they're going to expect this every time,'" Hamilton said.

Later, Hamilton admitted that he got caught up in the attention. Michigan–Notre Dame is a huge setting, and winning the game, especially in that fashion, gives you instant notoriety. He read everything written about him.

He lost his kicking rhythm, and two weeks after that memorable kick, coach Gary Moeller reminded him the starting job was not his. Hamilton went back to work. He finished his career having made 63 field goals for the Wolverines.

70 Mark Messner

Mark Messner was not the biggest defensive lineman to wear a Michigan uniform. Not that the 6'4", 235-pounder was small, of course, but Messner was more about quickness, smarts, and instincts than brawn and brute strength.

He was an explosive down lineman who, after redshirting his freshman year in 1984, started all 49 games of his career and led the Wolverines in sacks in 1985, 1986, and 1987.

"I am not real big, and I am not real strong," Messner said during his Michigan days. "I try to avoid people rather than take them on."

Really? Is that how he explained the gaudy defensive statistics he produced during his career?

Actually, his point was that he avoided offensive linemen, who often outweighed him by a solid 40 or 50 pounds, as he zeroed in on his target, the quarterback.

"I try to move with quickness toward his weakness," Messner said of opposing linemen. "I try to get away from where he is leaning, like a matador steps around a bull."

Messner was a two-time All-American, and he remains Michigan's all-time leader in sacks with 36—the next closest is Brandon Graham, who had 29.5 career sacks from 2006 to 2009—and tackles for loss with 70—Graham is second on the list with 56 during his career. He remains the program's career leader in tackles-for-loss yardage (376), most single-game sacks with five against Northwestern on October 31, 1987, and most career sack yardage (273).

Messner was named MVP of the 1986 Fiesta Bowl after registering nine tackles, forcing a fumble, and recovering another in the Wolverines' 27–23 victory over Nebraska.

Michigan All-America tackle Mark Messner jokes during a workout at Orange Coast Community College in December 1988 prior to the Wolverines' Rose Bowl game against USC.

He used his redshirt year to learn the college game and prepare himself to compete for a starting job the next fall. Messner competed hard through August training camp and earned his way onto the Wolverines' defensive line as the starting left end. His first career start would come against No. 13 Notre Dame at Michigan Stadium. There's no doubt that during that first season, Messner benefited greatly from playing on the line with All-American Mike Hammerstein.

Opposing teams would avoid running to Hammerstein's side and focus on going after the redshirt freshman, Messner. "Having Hammer on the line with me was helpful because it took a lot of pressure off me," Messner said. "Everyone was focused on him, and that enabled me to get some action going toward me. They'd double-team him and come out after me."

Remarkably, Messner finished his season as a third-team All-American for the Wolverines, who finished ranked No. 2 nationally. He was shocked by the national individual honor.

"I originally thought it might be a mistake, because they don't usually put first-year players on the list," Messner said. "I suppose since I snuck up on people during the season that it's only logical I'd sneak onto the All-American team."

Messner's goal throughout his four-year career at Michigan was to play with "youthful intensity" like "a young kid."

A young kid with plenty of smarts and terrific instincts.

71 Jamie Morris: Talented Tailback

It wasn't that Bo Schembechler thought Jamie Morris wasn't tough enough or didn't have the ability to play tailback at Michigan—after all, Morris came from a strong line of football players, including older brother Joe, who was Syracuse's all-time leading rusher and went on to an NFL career with the New York Giants—but he was small.

Morris, a 5'7" tailback, arrived in Ann Arbor in 1984 weighing 150 pounds. Oh, sure, he had the size to cut it in the Big Ten against bruising opponents. Well, at least that's what he told Schembechler.

Schembechler wanted Morris to return kicks. Morris wanted to run the ball. Before practice started that fall, Morris walked into Schembechler's office and asked if he could play tailback.

"We'll see," Schembechler told him.

Later at practice, the coaches called the players and told them to join their position groups. Morris was told to join the backs.

Despite his diminutive stature, Jamie Morris left big footprints in Michigan tailback lore. Photo courtesy of Per Kjeldsen.

During the scrimmage that day, Morris had a 15-yard run and was hit hard by cornerback Garland Rivers, proving to the coaches he could withstand the punishment.

Schembechler would joke later that he did tell Morris during that meeting that he would give him a chance to "try" to be a running back at Michigan.

"Good thing I did, isn't it?" Schembechler said, laughing.

Morris' role as kick-return specialist did not last long. In the third game of his freshman season, with tailbacks Rick Rogers and Gerald White injured, Schembechler inserted Morris as the starting tailback. He maintained the starting role throughout his career, from 1984 to 1987, and that season he became the first freshman since Wally Teninga in 1945 to lead the team in rushing.

He set Michigan's single-season rushing record with 1,703 yards in 1987, and he was the all-time career rushing leader with 4,392 yards. Both of those records were broken 13 years later by Anthony Thomas.

One record that has withstood the test of time is Morris' career all-purpose-yardage total of 6,201. Until Mike Hart (2004–2007), Morris was the only player in Michigan history to lead the Wolverines in rushing each of his four seasons. Morris was sure-handed as well, and had 99 receptions for 756 yards and 51 kickoff returns for 1,027 yards.

Morris distinguished himself as a tailback who grew stronger the more carries he had in a game.

"The thing about him is, if you give him enough carries, he gives you your game's worth," Schembechler said at the time about Morris. "I used to take him out after two or three carries, and he'd get mad."

While his older brother Joe was more of a hard-nosed, run-at-you type of back, Morris had great finesse as a runner.

"My strength is being flashy, cutting and slashing," Morris said.

He will be remembered for his game against Ohio State in 1986, when he rushed for 210 yards—he had 302 all-purpose—to help lead the Wolverines and back up quarterback Jim Harbaugh's guarantee in a 26–24 victory.

He finished his Michigan career with a flourish. Morris, who captained the 1987 team with Doug Mallory, ran for a career-best 234 yards—the best bowl performance by a Michigan back—to help lead Michigan to a 28–24 win over Alabama in the Hall of Fame Bowl. Morris shared Most Valuable Player honors with Alabama's Bobby Humphrey.

After the game, Morris spoke to Schembechler by phone, since the coach was home recovering from quadruple-heart-bypass surgery.

"He told me, 'You looked like a bull out there,'" Morris said.

Good thing Schembechler let the bull try to play running back at Michigan, isn't it?

72 Bob Ufer: Legendary Radio Voice of UM Football

For so many seasons, year after year, Bob Ufer was the voice of Michigan football.

Ufer was clever and endearing, enthusiastic and loyal, and first and foremost a Michigan fan. The former Michigan athlete, a track and field star who set eight freshman records and in 1942 set the indoor world record in the 440, called 363 consecutive Michigan games from 1945 to 1981.

He was authentic, an original whose "Uferisms" are still, long after his death, cherished by Wolverines fans.

Where does one begin? After all, there are 363 games to choose from and all those funny, amusing, and clearly heartfelt descriptions.

Ufer referred to Michigan as "Meeshegan," which he actually took from legendary coach Fielding H. Yost—that's how Yost pronounced the school name. Then there was the horn. It was the actual horn from General George Patton's jeep, a gift to Ufer from Patton's son. Ufer referred to Bo Schembechler as "George Patton Schembechler" and this was the "George Patton Schembechler Horn." Three honks meant a touchdown, two honks meant a field goal or safety, and one honk for an extra point.

He called the home games by referring to Michigan Stadium as the "hole that Yost dug, Canham carpeted, and Schembechler filled."

There is no doubt the always-enthusiastic Ufer became even more animated for the annual Michigan–Ohio State rivalry game.

Ufer referred to OSU coach Woody Hayes as "Dr. Strange Hayes," and he once referred to a crowd at Ohio Stadium as "10,000 alumni and 74,000 truck drivers."

Perhaps his wildest pre–Michigan–Ohio State call came in his pregame opening for the 1969 game as the top-ranked Buckeyes came into Ann Arbor.

"Yessir, it's finally here—Meeshegan versus Ohio State in football," Ufer bellowed. "Twenty minutes until blast-off as two of the oldest rivals in the Big Ten square off in the game of the day, the game of the year, the game of the decade. Call it what you will, it promises to be two and a half hours of some of the most exciting football in the 104-year history of man's inhumanity to man."

Another Ufer classic came in the minutes before kickoff of the 1973 Michigan–Ohio State game in Ann Arbor. The Buckeyes ran onto the field and went straight for the M Club banner—the banner touched by every Wolverine as he makes his way out of the tunnel toward the sideline. Ohio State players tore down the banner.

"They're tearing down Michigan's coveted M Club banner!" Ufer screamed. "They will meet a dastardly fate here for that! There isn't a Michigan Man who wouldn't like to go out and scalp those Buckeyes right now."

During the Michigan-Iowa game on October 17, 1981, Ufer's last broadcast, the Michigan marching band formed his name on the field in tribute. He passed away nine days later from cancer.

Ufer lives on, however. During the football season, radio stations frequently play some of the Ufer radio highlights during pregame shows, and during the rivalry weeks, particularly Michigan State and Ohio State, Ufer seems like a regular on radio.

A website created to honor Ufer—www.ufer.org—sells CDs with Ufer's great calls, Ufer bobbleheads, and if you can't get enough Ufer, there's always the Ufer ringtone for your cell phone.

73 Harry Kipke and His Nine Varsity Letters

Harry Kipke was as clever as he was dedicated and dominant on the football field.

After his playing days at Michigan (1921–1923), during which he lettered nine times in three different sports—football, basketball, and baseball—he was named head coach at Michigan in 1929.

During his tenure as coach, he was quoted in the *Saturday Evening Post* as humorously saying his system was "punt, pass, and a prayer," and he also coined the much-used phrase still used by coaches today: "A great defense is a great offense."

Before Kipke was being quoted in the country's great publications, he was making a name for himself in athletics at Michigan.

The 5'9", 155-pound Kipke played at halfback and punter for coach Fielding Yost, and still is considered one of Michigan's greatest punters because of his ability to punt out of bounds near the opponent's goal line. Michigan was 19–1–2 during Kipke's football career, and he was named All-America in 1922, captain of the 1923 team that won the national championship, going 8–0 and allowing its opponents a mere 12 points.

Perhaps his most dazzling performance came during the Michigan–Ohio State game on October 21, 1922, the day Ohio Stadium was officially dedicated. The stadium opened with a permanent seating capacity of 62,110 and temporary seating for 10,000, so the crowd was 72,000-plus.

Kipke was terrific at halfback and led the Wolverines to a 19–0 victory—it would be one of five shutouts that season. He scored both Michigan touchdowns, the first coming on a 26-yard change-of-direction play called "Old 83," Yost's favorite. The Wolverines worked out of the single-wing and Kipke started moving to the right side, then veered left. He took a shovel pass from quarterback Irwin Uteritz and scored.

He handed the ball to the official in the end zone and reportedly said, "Well, the place is really dedicated now."

Kipke's second touchdown was on a 38-yard interception return. He also made a 37-yard field goal and handled all the punting. He punted 11 times, including nine that went out of bounds inside the OSU 8-yard line.

Not forgetting his other athletic achievements, the Michigan basketball team was 36–15 during Kipke's three seasons, and the baseball team won two Big Ten titles and posted a 56–13 record.

Kipke's love was football, though. He spent four seasons as an assistant at Missouri and then became head coach at—gasp!—Michigan State in 1928. The Spartans went 3–4–1 that year, and in 1929, he was named head coach of his alma mater.

It would not be a flawless coaching run. The Wolverines in 1928, the year before Kipke took over, went 3–4–1 under Tad Wieman. Kipke's team saw improvement and went 5–3–1, but finished in an eighth-place tie in the conference.

Things quickly turned around. Kipke led the Wolverines to four straight conference titles and back-to-back national championships in 1932 and 1933.

But in 1934 the Wolverines endured a huge fall to 1–7 overall and 0–6 in the conference. From 1934 to 1937, Michigan struggled mightily and went 10–22 during those years. Kipke was fired, a move that surprised him because he reportedly had been informed he would be Michigan's coach the next season.

That opened the door for Fritz Crisler to take over as head coach, but to Kipke's credit, he did recruit many of the players, including Tom Harmon, Forest Evashevski, and Bob Westfall, who would have fabulous college careers. Kipke had encouraged a hedging Harmon to remain committed to Michigan even though he had been fired as head coach.

Kipke later served as a member of the university's board of regents and is a member of the National Football Hall of Fame and Michigan Hall of Fame.

74 The Mad Magicians

Michigan's star halfback, Bob Chappuis, was a member of Fritz Crisler's famed "Mad Magicians," a group that ran one of the trickiest, most precise, most mind-boggling offenses in college football.

In 1947 the Wolverines, as a group, were fairly small. The largest player weighed 220 pounds, and the offensive line averaged about 182 pounds. Teams across the country had started moving toward the T formation, but Crisler, who was 48 and had spent the last 18 years as a coach, would not budge.

Crisler and the Wolverines stuck with the razzle-dazzle of the single-wing. For one thing, player size was not an issue in that offense. This offense was about precision, skill, and quickness, and Crisler would make the team drill for hours in order to achieve perfection.

There was much to learn. Crisler had devised 170 play variations—double-reverses, buck-reverse laterals, crisscrosses, quick hits, and spins from seven formations, and the ball would change hands several times.

Michigan's backfield in 1947 featured Howard Yerges at quarterback, Bump Elliott and Chappuis at halfback, and Jack Weisenberger at fullback. Dick Rifenburg and Bob Mann were the ends, Don Tomasi and Stu Wilkins the guards, Bruce Hilkene and Bill Pritula the tackles, and J.T. White the center.

Just how complicated was it? Try this on for size.

"We had one play where the fullback took the ball from center and handed it to the upback, who pitched it to me," Chappuis said.

"I handed it to [Bump] Elliott, and he handed it to the end, who threw it to the other end. The ball was touched by seven people!"

It was a special team, one, the players said many years later, that worked so well because it was so tight-knit. And the Mad Magicians were magical mainly because of Crisler and his demanding ways.

"We did rehearse until he was satisfied, until we knew what we were doing and how to do it," Chappuis said. "If he would see one thing that didn't fit the picture, he would make us continue to work until we got it right."

One day in practice, things just weren't going right. Crisler was miffed. "Let's quit," Crisler barked at the team. "You'll never get it done right." Practice ended on that note. The next day, the Wolverines pleaded with Crisler to let them have another chance to perfect the offense. The rest, as they say, is history.

By the end of the regular season, the Wolverines were 9–0, Big Nine champions, and ranked No. 2. They outscored teams 345–53, including four shutouts.

The Mad Magicians made their biggest splash on New Year's Day 1948, in the Rose Bowl. Michigan defeated USC in a 49–0 rout, and after a second poll was taken by the AP voters, the Wolverines became national champions.

Crisler was so sure that USC would try to handcuff his offense, not only did he have the scouting notes taken diligently by 1940 Michigan Heisman Trophy winner Tom Harmon, who scouted six USC regular-season games for Crisler, but he added some new wrinkles.

Michigan added a formation in which all the linemen were on one side of the center, except one guard. They also used a shift in the line, which they had not used before.

"I thought it would confuse them a bit," Crisler said in a 1979 interview.

After the team had returned from the Rose Bowl, Michigan students got a copy of the game film and showed it at Hill Auditorium. The players were asked to narrate the film.

"Half the time we didn't know who was handling the ball, and we'd end up using the wrong names," Chappuis said. "And often, the camera would miss the play."

If you want to see for yourself what the Mad Magicians were all about, there is a six-minute film clip online at YouTube.com from the 1948 Rose Bowl. That clip offers a glimpse at just how technical and challenging the offense truly was.

75 The Game 1950: The Snow Bowl

The 1950 Michigan–Ohio State game in Columbus, known as the Snow Bowl, was a magnificent display of...punting.

Columbus had been pounded the night before and into the morning of the game by the worst blizzard it had ever endured. In some parts, there were two feet of snow. Ohio State athletics director Dick Larkins and Michigan athletics director Fritz Crisler weren't even certain the game should be played, but with 50,503 fans braving the 10-degree temperatures, the game went on. Also a factor was the fact that had the game been canceled, Ohio State would have gone to the Rose Bowl by default. Larkins reportedly didn't want to win that way, and Crisler wanted to play.

Certainly, it was memorable.

The field was barely visible from the stands and press box, let alone by the players, and the game was delayed 20 minutes as workmen tried to clear the field. But why bother? For what? To watch a punting exhibition?

There were 45 combined punts—Michigan's Chuck Ortmann punted 24 times for 723 yards and Ohio State's Vic Janowicz 21 times for 672 yards—and the teams often opted to punt on first, second, or third down, hoping the return team would fumble near its own end zone. Ultimately, punting was the only strategy because trying to move the ball in those conditions and on a snow-covered field was ridiculously hopeless. Ohio State made three first downs, while Michigan never made one. Michigan attempted nine passes, never completing one. Still, the Wolverines prevailed 9–3 for the Big Ten title and a trip to the Rose Bowl.

Ohio State scored first after Bob Momsen recovered a blocked kick, and Janowicz kicked a field goal. Michigan's first score came when Al Wahl blocked a Janowicz kick that rolled out of the end zone for a safety. The Wolverines had cut the lead to 3–2.

With 47 seconds left in the first half, Ohio State faced third down at its 4-yard line. Michigan called a timeout. OSU coach Wes Fesler decided to punt on third down. Janowicz's punt was blocked by Tony Momsen, Bob's brother. Momsen went after the ball, which was dancing into the snow-covered end zone. He dove for the ball, but it slipped away. Momsen dove again, and this time he cradled it in the end zone for the game's only touchdown. Harry Allis kicked the extra point.

The rest of the game was about the finer art of punting in miserable game conditions.

"It was like a nightmare," Janowicz said after the game. "My hands were numb. I had no feeling in them, and I don't know how I hung onto the ball. It was terrible. You knew what you wanted to do, but you couldn't do it."

Michigan was grateful to escape with the victory against the more-talented Buckeyes.

"Imagine having a great team like Fesler had and then not being able to use it because of the conditions," Michigan coach Bennie Oosterbaan said. "Naturally, I'm happy to have won, but the conditions were such that it wasn't a fair test of football."

Janowicz went on to win the Heisman Trophy that year, and Michigan won the Rose Bowl.

76 Ron Johnson: A Magical Day

There have been great tailbacks throughout Michigan history. Great ones. Some have been consistently strong season after season, some became more seasoned as they got older and saved their best for last, and others provided memorable individual performances that even decades later, Michigan fans can relate with crystal-clear recall.

Maybe you were at the 1968 Michigan-Wisconsin game on November 16, 1968. Probably not. Michigan Stadium was half full that day, only 51,117 attended, but like many spectacular events throughout history, the number of people who really, truly witnessed it grows and grows over the years.

Ron Johnson, a Detroit-native, provided that singular performance on what he would later call a "magical day," his final game at Michigan Stadium.

With his parents sitting in University of Michigan school president Robben Fleming's box, Johnson rushed for 347 yards on 31 carries to lead the Wolverines to a 34–9 victory, their eighth straight that season. Johnson scored five times on runs of 35, 67, 1, 60, and 49 yards. Johnson's 347 yards broke Heisman Trophy winner Tom Harmon's record. That mark set an NCAA record at the time and remains a Michigan single-game rushing record. Johnson could have added to that total, but he removed himself from the game in the fourth quarter to give backup Lance Scheffler some playing time.

Johnson captained the Wolverines in 1968, and they finished 8–2 overall and second in the Big Ten.

Johnson, who graduated from Michigan's business school with a concentration in finance, later became chairman of the National Football Foundation and College Hall of Fame, but it is that 347-yard game that he always is asked about.

"I couldn't believe it," Johnson said later in an interview. "When I got off the field, the statistician came up to me and asked what I thought. I guessed, 250, but it was 347. When you look at that amount of yards, it really is an amazing feat."

Johnson still holds that record at Michigan, along with single-season records for most touchdowns with 19 and most touchdowns in a game, the five he scored that day against Wisconsin. He set a Big Ten rushing record with 1,021 yards in 1968 and was awarded the *Chicago Tribune*'s Silver Football as the league's Most Valuable Player.

He also set a Michigan single-season record with 1,391 yards and became Michigan's career rushing leader with 2,440.

Johnson finished sixth in the Heisman Trophy voting and was named an All-American. He also earned the Big Ten Medal, awarded to the outstanding scholar-athlete from each of the league's schools.

After his Michigan career ended, Johnson was a first-round pick of the Cleveland Browns and played seven years in the NFL, becoming an MVP running back for the New York Giants.

77 John Navarre: Taking Criticism and Leaving a Legacy

Describing the career of quarterback John Navarre is a challenge because he easily was one of the most scrutinized athletes in recent Michigan history.

He was thrust onto the scene a year earlier than scheduled, when Drew Henson left Michigan to pursue a career in Major League Baseball, and Navarre endured some very public growing pains on the field. By the time his career was over, he held all seven of Michigan's major career passing records and was named first team All–Big Ten. He had also endured more public criticism than any Michigan player in recent memory.

Navarre, quiet and patient, always maintained the high road. He never shot back at his critics among the media or the Michigan fan base. Perhaps more defining, he never gave up.

"I'm very glad I took that route," Navarre later said. "I didn't like a lot of the stuff, but it made me a stronger person. I took a lot of life lessons from it."

His coach didn't like it. At all. Lloyd Carr was frequently angered by the criticism of his quarterback who was considered to be too slow, threw the ball too hard, had too many balls knocked down, was inaccurate, and too stoic. Anything else?

Carr was beside himself with praise, frequently calling Navarre an "unbelievable human being" who had to weather more than most.

"The way he handled all of the things that were said about him and written about him…. I can't tell you how much I admire him," Carr said. "I have had some quarterbacks here. I mean, great ones. John Navarre is one of them."

Certainly, it wasn't easy for Navarre. His sophomore season in 2001 was a challenge on many levels. Michigan finished 8–4, including a 26–20 loss to Ohio State in which Navarre threw four interceptions. He visited Carr in his office after the bowl game.

Carr spoke bluntly. "I looked at him and I said, 'John, you think you know what you're going to go through, but it's going to be even worse,'" Carr said. "So before we even addressed the challenge, he had to decide if he wanted to go through it. He didn't hesitate. He said, 'Yes, I do.'"

His teammates rallied around Navarre, as well. They said the criticism served to drive him.

"As a young person, getting bashed publicly in front of America is difficult," Navarre's roommate Tony Pape said. "You're 20 years old, and you have people telling you you're terrible and that you don't belong there. Nobody deserves that."

Navarre defined his career during his senior season in 2003. Michigan and Navarre, a cocaptain that season, struggled in losses at Oregon and Iowa, and he endured the knock for being winless in six games against ranked teams in road games.

At Minnesota, he orchestrated a brilliant 21-point comeback, as the Wolverines scored 31 in the fourth quarter to win. Finally, a win for Navarre against a ranked team on the road.

And then, the real test. Michigan would face Ohio State in the 100th meeting between the two rivals, this time at Michigan Stadium before a record crowd. This would be Navarre's opportunity to leave his legacy. After all, he entered The Game with an 0–2 record against the hated Buckeyes.

That week he was asked repeatedly how he would be remembered if Michigan didn't beat Ohio State. What would be his legacy? What would it be? Navarre sidestepped the question diplomatically, and then on game day he went to work. Navarre was 21-of-32 for 278 yards and two touchdowns, including a 64-yarder, the longest of his career, as he helped lead the Wolverines to a 35–21 victory.

Navarre had tears in his eyes as he addressed the media after the game. He also slightly admonished those who suggested his Michigan legacy had been on the line that day.

"The reality was, that's how the media saw it," he said. "I felt established."

Michigan finished that regular season 10–2 and as Big Ten champions.

Carr, again, let loose on Navarre's critics after the Wolverines' victory over Ohio State. "I have no problem with criticism," Carr said. "I'm talking about people who went overboard, who wrote and said things about John Navarre to humiliate, embarrass, and degrade him. I thought some of the things were absolutely despicable."

Until Chad Henne shattered the Michigan record books, Navarre held season records for passing yards (3,331), pass attempts (456), and completions (270).

78 John Wangler: Just Throwing

How is John Wangler best remembered? As one of Michigan's most efficient quarterbacks and a guy who helped lead the Wolverines to a Big Ten title and a win over Ohio State in 1980, or as half of the Wangler-to–Anthony Carter duo? Really, it makes no difference to him.

Truthfully, Wangler feels like a lucky man to have played quarterback at Michigan, considering he was a drop-back passer in the era of Bo Schembechler, who as most know, really liked to run and run the option.

"I don't think Bo envisioned me as his quarterback," Wangler said.

Wangler believes he benefited from a time when Michigan and Ohio State would recruit certain players just so they wouldn't have to play against them. Michigan assistant coach Bill McCartney was the one who pushed Schembechler to sign Wangler.

With receiver Anthony Carter at Michigan as a freshman in 1979, Wangler arriving to fill the void left by Rick Leach, and a solid offensive line, the Wolverines had plenty of weapons.

"Pick your poison," Wangler said. "It was very easy. I could do it on one leg."

He was joking, really.

Wangler literally was left with one good leg after the 1979 Gator Bowl against North Carolina. Michigan had taken a 9–0 lead after Wangler hit Carter on a 53-yard pass, but Michigan missed the extra point. On the next series, Wangler suffered a severe knee injury thanks to UNC linebacker Lawrence Taylor. He had thrown for 203 yards in the first half before being sidelined.

There was some thought during the offseason among the Michigan faithful that Wangler would not be able to return for his final season in 1980 because of the injury. But Wangler went through eight months of torturous rehabilitation to work his knee back into playing shape.

Rich Hewlett started the season opener against Northwestern, a 17–10 win, but Notre Dame was the following week on the road. Wangler was still listed as No. 2 on the depth chart

Notre Dame took a 7–0 lead early in the second quarter, which quickly expanded to 14–0. Schembechler needed to do something to better utilize Carter, the Wolverines' biggest weapon.

"I looked down the sidelines at Johnny Wangs," Schembechler recalled in his book. "He knew what I was thinking. 'Can you go, Wangs?' 'I can go, Coach.'"

Schembechler next said the unthinkable—he told Wangler to throw. "I need you to throw, you got it?" Schembechler said. "Throw. Just throw!"

Schembechler then gathered the offensive linemen and told them under no circumstance could Wangler be touched.

"I didn't have to say more," Schembechler said. "You could see the look in their eyes. They loved Johnny Wangs. I mean, absolutely adored him. They would have blocked a tank if necessary. Wangs went into that game and led one of the gutsiest comebacks I have ever witnessed."

With 1:45 left in the half and Wangler directing the offense, Michigan pulled to 14–7. Notre Dame chose not to run out the clock and that proved costly, as Marion Body made the interception and returned it to the Notre Dame 27 with 1:30 left. With 31 seconds left, after Michigan had faked a field-goal attempt to reach the 9-yard line, Wangler hit Norm Betts for a game-tying touchdown.

Michigan took the lead 27–26 with 41 seconds left but failed to make a two-point conversion after Wangler led another scoring drive. Notre Dame made a miraculous final drive and perhaps more miraculous, Harry Oliver made a 51-yard field goal to win 29–27.

The Wolverines finished 10–2 overall and 8–0 in the Big Ten to earn the Rose Bowl bid. Michigan gave Schembechler his first Rose Bowl victory, a 23–6 win against Washington.

"We were lucky to be coached by Bo," Wangler said. "To have Bo in that era, it was amazing, truly amazing. Every day you couldn't wait to get to practice. You couldn't wait to get coached by the guy. It was hard, don't get me wrong. But I can't tell you there wasn't one day I didn't love going down there and being around him and those guys."

79 The 1970 Rose Bowl and Bo's Heart Attack

Michigan and its first-year coach Bo Schembechler were on an incredible high. The Wolverines had upset the nation's No. 1 team, Ohio State, in stunning fashion at Michigan Stadium in the 1969 regular-season finale, and it was on to the Rose Bowl.

Schembechler, 40, had never been to a bowl game, and after beating OSU, there was no time to rest as he and the team began preparations to face USC on New Year's Day. The journey was difficult and tiring. Schembechler and his staff not only had to game-plan for the bowl game, but they had to get established in recruiting and were on the road wooing high school seniors. All of that was taking its toll on Schembechler, who within the year since he had been hired at Michigan gained 25 pounds.

Two days before the Rose Bowl, Schembechler started to feel a bit odd. He had a pain in his chest, and under doctors' orders, he rested and gave defensive assistant Jim Young the job of handling the final news conference the next day. He took an echocardiogram at a hospital in Pasadena, but it was negative. Schembechler was relieved…and hungry, so we went back to the hotel and ordered two hamburgers.

The Michigan team had moved to a monastery in the San Gabriel hills to escape the craziness of the pre-bowl scene. Schembechler and his wife, Millie, a nurse, remained at the hotel. Still, there was a final practice, and there was no way he would miss it.

Typically, he was a fiery and demanding coach who loved practice and loved work, but the day before the Rose Bowl, he found it difficult to get motivated. So what did he do? He essentially put himself through drills. He took a football and began running sprints, and he ran them hard from hash mark to hash mark. Schembechler knew he needed to find the energy to coach, and this is how he knew to find it.

He later admitted he still felt lethargic.

That night, the eve of the Rose Bowl, the priests at the house at the bottom of the hill where the players were staying held a small party for the coaches. They encouraged Schembechler to drink a soft drink to calm his stomach. That didn't work.

Meanwhile, Michigan president Robben Fleming had arrived at the monastery to speak to the team, and Schembechler was asked to join them. He started to climb the hill to the guest house when he was struck with chest pain. In a later description, Schembechler said he stopped and held on to a tree because the pain was so intense. But he managed to reach his destination and introduced Fleming to the team. Schembechler went to bed early, not making his usual stops, like meeting with his assistant coaches, something they found completely unusual for their perfectionist boss.

The morning of the game, he awoke with a headache and felt awful. His assistants, who had been alarmed by his behavior the night before, asked the team doctors to take a look at him again. At the hospital, while awaiting another test, he studied his play chart for the game. He was then informed by the head of cardiology at St. Luke's that he would be "out of the game," that he had suffered a heart attack and needed to be placed in intensive care.

"I cried," Schembechler said later, recalling that morning. "I had all my life prepared for this hour. I never got to coach it. At first thought, I'm 40 years old and just getting started in my career. Would I be able to coach again?"

Schembechler met briefly with his assistants and told Young he would coach the team. The Wolverines, knowing what their coach was going through, looked as though they were in a fog that day. Michigan lost 10–3.

He would remain in the hospital for 18 days and read every book about the heart and heart attacks that he could find. Schembechler also received a number of letters. Among them, one from his mentor, Ohio State coach Woody Hayes:

"Dear Bo: If you were going to have a sick spell, why didn't you have it at our game, for your team didn't look the same without you." He signed it, "Your old coach and longtime friend, Woody."

80 Bo Finally Wins the Rose Bowl

In the days leading up to the 1981 Rose Bowl, the focus wasn't exactly on Michigan and Washington. No, most of the attention was on Michigan coach Bo Schembechler, who had taken five Michigan teams to the Rose Bowl but had nothing to show for it in the win column.

Oh-and-five. It stung. Not only were Schembechler's teams winless in the Rose Bowl, but the Wolverines also had lost in the Orange and Gator Bowls.

The national media picked on Schembechler, poked fun, and cracked bad jokes. It was a monkey, all right, maybe even a gorilla, and the Wolverines wanted whatever it was off their backs.

"We want to win for our coach as much as for ourselves," UM center George Lilja said before the game.

Even the players joked.

"If we win, maybe it'll look good on our résumé when we go in to apply for a regular job," said Andy Cannavino, a cocaptain. "Maybe the boss will be sympathetic to the fact that we got Bo Schembechler his first Rose Bowl."

In the end, Michigan won 23–6 over Washington, and the Wolverines kicked the monkey off and instead carried Schembechler on their shoulders. He later called that bowl game his "most satisfying."

Schembechler had made news before the 1970 Rose Bowl, his first as Michigan head coach, when he was hospitalized with a heart attack and could not coach. After his first Rose Bowl victory, Schembechler emerged from the field with a bloody nose, accidentally inflicted by one of his players during the celebration.

"By the time I got pounded on out there, I could hardly breathe," he said, laughing. "And I don't have the best of hearts."

He admitted to shedding a few tears after the win.

Michigan's defense played remarkably well. They kept Washington out of the end zone and preserved a streak of not allowing an offensive touchdown for 22 straight quarters.

Early in the game, the Huskies reached the Michigan 1-yard line, but the Wolverines made a critical fourth-down stop. The teams were scoreless in the first quarter. Washington got on the board first with Chuck Nelson's 35-yard field goal, but Michigan took the lead on a six-yard touchdown run by Butch Woolfolk. Nelson added another field goal, and Michigan took a 7–6 lead into halftime—the first time a Schembechler-coached team led at halftime of a Rose Bowl.

Bo and his team celebrate their 1981 Rose Bowl win in the locker room after the game. Photo courtesy of Per Kjeldsen.

Michigan's standout receiver Anthony Carter did not catch a pass in the first half, and quarterback John Wangler, who had told the coaches at halftime that he didn't want to force throws to a double-covered Carter, was told to, well, force them.

Carter caught a 27-yard pass from Wangler to the Washington 11-yard line during Michigan's first possession of the second half. Four plays later, Michigan took a 10–6 lead on a 25-yard field goal by Ali Haji-Sheikh to end an 83-yard drive.

Schembechler would later call that opening drive the turning point of the game.

"To take that kick and drive down the field on them, I think might have taken something out of them," he said.

On Michigan's next possession, the Wolverines went to the air, as Wangler completed passes of 10, 17, and 14 yards, before connecting on a seven-yard touchdown pass to Carter for the 17–6 lead. The Wolverines sealed the victory on a one-yard touchdown run by Stan Edwards with 4:02 left in the game.

199

The Wolverines shut down the Washington offense in the second half, outgaining the Huskies 304–105.

"They kept getting better," Washington coach Don James said of Michigan's defense.

Woolfolk gained 182 yards on 26 carries and was named Rose Bowl Most Valuable Player. Carter finished with 101 yards of total offense.

Schembechler finally had his elusive Rose Bowl victory, the first for Michigan since 1965.

"I've been here five times, and five times I sat here with my head between my legs," Schembechler said in his postgame news conference. "Now I can smoke a cigar and enjoy it.... I'm on top of the world in every respect."

81 Michigan–Notre Dame 1978: Rivalry Rekindled

The plan to resume the Michigan–Notre Dame series was hatched late in 1968 during a football banquet in Detroit when Notre Dame athletics director Moose Krause approached Michigan athletics director Don Canham.

Canham knew about the issues former Michigan coach Fritz Crisler had with the Notre Dame series and why the game was dropped, but Canham was a marketer, and he wanted Michigan Stadium filled and the athletics department to generate money.

Bringing back the Michigan–Notre Dame rivalry didn't seem like a bad idea. "I can't take credit for being an emancipator or anything like that," Canham said in John Kryk's book *Natural Enemies*. "I mean, it was strictly a financial decision. I had one hell of a headache trying to balance the budget, and the first thing I did was try to beef up the schedule so we drew some people."

Michigan faced Notre Dame in 1978, the first meeting between the natural rivals in 35 years. The game was not without a number of storylines.

Rick Leach, Michigan's senior quarterback and by his coach Bo Schembechler's account a legitimate Heisman Trophy candidate, injured his foot and didn't practice Tuesday and Wednesday of that week. This was a game Leach had circled since his freshman year—he was going to find a way to play, even though Schembechler had an unwritten rule that if a player doesn't practice, he doesn't play.

Meanwhile, Notre Dame coach Dan Devine had his Fighting Irish dress in their special green jerseys, the ones they wore the previous year when they trounced USC 49–19. Notre Dame, although a 3–0 loser to Missouri in its game two weeks earlier, was a one-point favorite over Michigan at Notre Dame Stadium.

Leach convinced Schembechler he should and would play, and after a slow first half, he brought the Wolverines to life in the second half, throwing three touchdowns in a 28–14 victory. Leach was 3-of-14 in the first half, and the Irish led 14–7, but in the second half, he was 5-of-6 for 89 yards and scored those three touchdowns.

"The story of the game was the second half," Schembechler said after the game. "I felt if we could get back in the game in the second half, the momentum would swing our way. We don't often trail at halftime like that. The thing was, to come out and keep at 'em. There were a lot of kids out there who played their guts out that second half. A lot. We will not wilt physically. All I know is we played Notre Dame, and we won."

Notre Dame committed five second-half turnovers, including three that led to touchdowns. Leach hit tight end Doug Marsh with a six-yard touchdown pass to tie the score 14–14 late in the third quarter. He found Marsh again on a 17-yard pass midway through the fourth quarter to give Michigan the lead 20–14—Gregg Willner's extra-point attempt was blocked. Ralph Clayton scored the third touchdown of the half on a 40-yard pass from Leach with 9:18 to go for the 26–14 lead. Joe Montana, Notre Dame's quarterback, was tackled in the end zone for a safety late in the game.

Michigan running back Harlan Huckleby rushed for a game-high 96 yards, though he sat out much of the second quarter. He rushed for 67 yards in the second half.

Notre Dame's Jerome Heavens made it clear after the game that he was not overly impressed by the Wolverines. "I'm not taking anything away from Michigan, but I really don't think they were that tough," he said.

82 The 1,000ᵗʰ Game: Michigan vs. Minnesota

One thousand games. *One thousand.*

Examine that chunk of football history and what comes across, ultimately, is that Michigan has so often set the standard in college football. Through those 1,000 games, Michigan had seen coaching legends Fielding H. Yost, Fritz Crisler, and Bo Schembechler at its helm. Through those 1,000 games, Michigan had seen a program move from Regents Field to "the Big House," Michigan Stadium.

From very humble beginnings, a 1–0 victory over Racine in 1879 before 500 fans, to a 63–13 victory over Minnesota on October 24, 1992, before 106,579 on homecoming at Michigan Stadium, the Michigan football program established itself among the nation's elite.

That dominating victory gave Michigan its 728ᵗʰ victory in 113 years of competition. The Wolverines had, including the victory that day against Minnesota, outscored their opponents, 23,935–9,316 during those 1,000 games.

And just for good measure, the Little Brown Jug, the trophy awarded to the winner of the Michigan-Minnesota game, remained in Ann Arbor for another year. The Wolverines had defeated the Gophers six straight years.

There were several milestones achieved on the day Michigan commemorated its 1,000th game. Quarterback Elvis Grbac broke Jim Harbaugh's career passing record after completing 14-of-19 for 208 yards and four touchdowns. He finished that game with 5,614 career yards, 165 yards past Harbaugh's mark.

Grbac and receiver Derrick Alexander connected for three touchdowns in the first quarter against Minnesota—they were catches of 52, 13, and three yards—and built a 21–7 lead. Grbac hit Alexander on a 32-yard touchdown pass in the third quarter. Alexander finished with seven catches for 130 yards, and he became the first Michigan player to catch four touchdown passes in a game.

Michigan took a 7–0 lead when Grbac found Alexander down the left side for the 52-yard touchdown run, but Minnesota answered right away when John Lewis returned the kickoff 88 yards. The Wolverines scored on their second possession when, on third-and-3, Grbac found Alexander on a corner route to the left side for the 17-yard score and a 14–7 lead.

The Wolverines continued to roll efficiently in the first quarter. On their third possession of the quarter, Michigan started at the Minnesota 47-yard line. Alexander caught his third touchdown of the game on a fade pattern to the right side.

Minnesota's only other score came early in the third quarter when Lewis caught a 94-yard pass from quarterback Marquel Fleetwood, but by then, the Wolverines were well ahead 35–13.

With the victory, the Wolverines equaled a Big Ten record with their 17th straight conference victory, a mark that Ohio State had accomplished three times.

Michigan was ranked third nationally entering the game against the lowly Gophers. The Wolverines remained at No. 3 after the dominating win that improved their record to 6–0–1, their only blemish at the time a 17–17 game at Notre Dame in the season opener. Minnesota left Ann Arbor at 1–6 overall, 1–3 in the Big Ten.

For the Wolverines, who did not score in the fourth quarter and saw their final three touchdowns come on the ground by Walter Smith, Tyrone Wheatley, and Che Foster, there were few errors in their 1,000th game. They scored on nine of their first 11 possessions.

83 Don Canham: Athletics Director Extraordinaire

The great ones at Michigan have left legacies.

Where do you start with Don Canham, who was ahead of his time as a college athletics director? Canham used his business savvy, marketing know-how, and love for the university to help lift it from its lull in attendance at Michigan Stadium, while putting the maize-and-blue colors, the "Michigan" name, and the Block "M" on apparel and merchandise available all over the country. Talk about name recognition.

Canham, a high-jumper while attending Michigan, later became the track coach before succeeding Fritz Crisler in 1968 as the athletics director. After expressing reluctance at taking the job because he had his own private business to run, Canham remained athletics director for 20 years.

"I turned it down [initially]," Canham told the *Michigan Daily*, the school's student newspaper, in a 2004 interview. "I had no ambition to become athletics director. Some of the other coaches… came to me and said, 'Look, take the interview, and if they give you the job, just do it for five years.'"

He took the job and immediately set a course to overhaul the Michigan football program. Bump Elliott became head coach in 1959 and had five losing seasons before retiring after the 1968 season. Attendance at Michigan Stadium, now over 100,000 capacity, had dipped considerably.

Elliott became associate athletics director under Canham, and the two searched for a coach. Joe Paterno wasn't interested, but the next man offered the job, Bo Schembechler of Miami (Ohio) and a former assistant under Woody Hayes at Ohio State, accepted. In December 1968 Canham announced Schembechler as the new head coach. Canham offered him a $21,000 salary that first year, and the deal was sealed on a handshake.

"I was impressed with Schembechler after 15 minutes," Canham later wrote. "He was exactly what I was looking for, someone who was very self-assured, tough, and had head-coaching experience."

With his coach in place, Canham could get to work reviving a sagging fan base. Michigan Stadium's capacity at the time was 101,001, but it had not been filled since 1955. He aggressively attacked this task, tirelessly working at finding ways to attract old and new fans.

"The first thing I did was I contacted every high school coach in the state of Michigan," Canham told the *Daily*. "I said, 'This fall, play on Friday nights, then on Saturday come to Ann Arbor.' We had five and six thousand high school football players come a week."

He was creative, to say the least.

Canham invited high school bands to fill the stadium. He enlisted the help of the San Diego Chicken and had Clydesdale

---

Finding Rare Air

Former Michigan coach Lloyd Carr has always been an avid reader, so it should not have come as any surprise that he drew inspiration for himself and his team in 1997 from the best-selling book *Into Thin Air.*

Carr contacted Lou Kasischke, who survived the tragic ascent of Mount Everest that was detailed in the book. Kasischke lived nearby in Bloomfield Hills, Michigan.

The Sunday night before Michigan opened that magical season, Kasischke spent nearly three hours with the Wolverines, describing the lessons of discipline, concentration, and teamwork, all lessons he learned from climbing the highest mountain in the world.

From that night on, the Wolverines treated their season as if on a climb. Carr gave each player a climbing pick bearing the player's name.

Later, Kasischke would say he was surprised by the depth of the questions he received from the Michigan players. They wanted to know about handling hardship and maintaining motivation.

"I knew they were understanding the messages from the Everest story," he said.

As Michigan neared a perfect regular season with Ohio State coming to town, Kasischke sent Carr prayer flags that had flown at the Everest base camp. The flags carried a Tibetan symbol that means "wind horse." As the wind blows the flag, the wind horse carries upward wishful words. Those flags flew at Michigan Stadium that day. Michigan won and finished an 11–0 season.

horses pay a visit. He marketed the games to women, inviting them to make a "picnic" out of a Saturday afternoon football game.

With Schembechler, an intense coach with one main desire—to beat his mentor at Ohio State—in place, Canham sought to make the Michigan–Ohio State game at Michigan Stadium a hot ticket. That game had not been sold out for 14 years, so what did Canham do? He advertised the game in Ohio and sold 23,000 tickets to Ohio fans for the 1969 game. Attendance for that game was 103,588, an enormous increase from the last time Michigan hosted The Game in 1967, when 64,144 attended.

Michigan famously upset top-ranked and unbeaten Ohio State 24–12 in 1969, the game that Schembechler later said put him and his program on the map.

"After we won, Bo came in and said, 'Don, don't ever do that [sell tickets to Ohioans] again,'" Canham said. "And I said, 'Now, I don't think I'll have to.'"

Canham made Saturdays at Michigan Stadium an experience people wanted to take part in. Fans began to tailgate with friends and family before *and* after games. It was all about the experience.

"We changed what a football game meant to people," he said. "We made it a spectacle, a carnival, a ball. We realized early that you can't always be No. 1 and can't advertise that, so we made Saturday an event."

From 1975 to the present day, Michigan has sold 100,000 or more tickets for every home game. It is the nation's attendance leader. Canham said he never imagined that kind of success at Michigan Stadium.

"The only thing I did know was that we were going to draw a hell of a lot more people than we ever did," he said in a *Daily* interview. "Up until then, schools did not advertise. I almost got fired when I flew a helicopter advertising Michigan football over the World Series [in Detroit] in 1968. That was considered undignified.

"We ran ads in magazines and all the Detroit suburban newspapers. Our big gimmick was that we mailed ticket applications—that first year we mailed 400,000 ticket applications and sold coffee cups and things like that. We paid for all the ads with the coffee cups. The premium we came up with paid for it all."

Canham retired from his post in 1988. He died in 2005. Michigan commemorated its dynamic athletics director by naming the school's swimming and diving facility, Canham Natatorium, after him.

84 Rich Rodriguez: First Hire outside of the "Bo" Lineage

Rich Rodriguez was introduced as the Michigan head coach on December 17, 2007, taking over for Lloyd Carr, who retired after 13 seasons in the job.

Rodriguez's stay, however, was short.

He was fired after three seasons and a 15–22 record, not to mention the Michigan football program's first NCAA investigation following a newspaper report just before the start of the 2009 season that quoted several players saying Rodriguez violated rules particularly involving practice time.

It was a challenging three years for Michigan fans, who endured a 3–9 record in 2008 and consecutive years without a bowl game—snapping a streak of 33 straight—and also for Rodriguez, who was hired, in part, because of his spread offense.

Rodriguez was the first Michigan coach hired since 1969 outside of the Bo Schembechler lineage of coaches, marking the first major coaching transition in the program—Schembechler has been succeeded by his assistant, Gary Moeller, who was then succeeded by Carr, who had been an assistant under both Moeller and Schembechler.

Rodriguez had spent the seven previous seasons coaching his alma mater West Virginia, before leaving there in the midst of controversy to take over the Wolverines. It never seemed to get any easier after his arrival in Ann Arbor.

He brought the spread to Michigan, but Michigan had always been a pro-style offense featuring a classic, drop-back quarterback. The first season was daunting, as the Wolverines finished 3–9, the worst in school history. The losing record broke Michigan's record of playing in 33 straight bowl games.

Before the start of the 2009 season, the *Detroit Free Press*, quoting anonymous players, indicated Rodriguez and his staff violated a number of rules. In February, 2010, the NCAA accused Michigan of five major rules violations.

Michigan admitted to four violations and self-imposed penalties, including cutting practice time and putting the program on two years of probation. Rodriguez and school president Mary Sue Coleman and athletic director Dave Brandon among others went to Seattle for a two-day hearing with the NCAA. The final report said the alleged infractions were less an issue than originally reported and Rodriguez was not found to have lost institutional control. An additional year of probation, however, was added.

That 2009 season, the Wolverines finished 5–7, again missing out on the postseason. The following year, with Denard Robinson leading the way at quarterback, Michigan started the season the same as it had the previous year, on a hot winning streak. The Wolverines were 5–0 but finished 7–5, including a 37–7 loss to Ohio State, and the defense was ranked among the nation's worst in NCAA statistics.

Michigan earned a trip to the Gator Bowl, but the off-field distractions were enormous and speculation was rampant that Rodriguez would be fired. Former Michigan players Jim Harbaugh, then at Stanford, and Les Miles, the LSU head coach, were among the names bandied about to replace Rodriguez.

The Wolverines suffered their worst-ever bowl loss, 52–14, to Mississippi State in the Gator Bowl on January 1, and four days later, Rodriguez was fired following two days of meetings with Brandon.

85 Comeback over Wisconsin in 2008

The booing was, well, really, really loud.

"Did I hear them?" Michigan coach Rich Rodriguez said, laughing after coaching in his first Big Ten contest. "If you were anywhere in the Ann Arbor vicinity, you heard 'em. I mean, holy cow, anybody would have heard that."

The Wolverines were trailing 19–0 at halftime against Wisconsin in the 2008 Big Ten opener for both teams. It was a half that featured five turnovers and only 21 yards of offense for the Wolverines, and fans were beginning to sense the team's first loss in a Big Ten opener at Michigan Stadium since 1967. Thus, the booing as the players and coaches trotted off the field and up the Michigan Stadium tunnel.

Perhaps it was the booing, maybe it was defensive tackle Terrance Taylor's emotional halftime speech, but the Michigan team that appeared in the second half was vastly different than the one that looked so miserable in the first in what was the program's 500th game at the Big House.

Michigan staged the biggest comeback in Michigan Stadium history to upset then–No. 9 Wisconsin 27–25. It was the Wolverines' 23rd straight Big Ten home-opening victory.

"I give all the credit in the world to Michigan to come back after hearing all the things that I heard being yelled at them at half-time," Wisconsin coach Bret Bielema said.

The entire coaching staff had not yet filtered into the locker room at halftime when Taylor decided to address his teammates. The uncensored version of the speech clearly was not tame and was aimed to motivate. Taylor said he was "very loud" and "very vocal."

"It was a lot of things," Taylor said. "Just the situation, my last year, my first, last Big Ten game at home, the 500th game, getting booed off the field.... I made sure I made eye contact with everybody in the room, because I was talking to everyone, offense included. Sometimes when you're down, and you don't have any momentum on the field, you can get down on yourself personally."

Taylor said the defense remained confident at halftime, knowing it had stifled the Badgers' red-zone production and held them to mostly field goals in the first half.

Wisconsin held its 19–0 advantage late into the third quarter when Michigan finally put together a scoring drive. The Wolverines went 80 yards in 14 plays, scoring on a 26-yard pass from Steven Threet to freshman tight end Kevin Koger with 2:22 left in the third quarter to cut the Badgers' lead to 19–7.

Michigan's next score, on an 85-yard drive kept alive by a roughing-the-passer penalty, was punctuated by Brandon Minor's 34-yard touchdown run. Michigan trailed 19–14 with 10:27 left in the game. The Wolverines took their first lead of the game three seconds later when linebacker John Thompson intercepted Allan Evridge's pass on the first play of Wisconsin's drive. He returned it 25 yards for a 20–19 lead, but Michigan failed on a two-point conversion.

Michigan took a 27–19 lead with 5:11 left when freshman Sam McGuffie scored on a three-yard run. With 13 seconds remaining, Evridge found David Gilreath in the end zone for the Badgers' final score. The Badgers' two-point conversion to tie the game was negated by a penalty for an illegal man downfield.

86 Michigan-Minnesota 2003: The Fourth-Quarter Comeback

The season, it appeared, was over. At least the national championship hopes were gone. Michigan was reeling after a loss to Iowa, its second in three games, was 4–2 overall and 1–1 in Big Ten play when the Wolverines headed to Minnesota for a Friday night game at the Metrodome in 2003. The Little Brown Jug, one of the oldest trophies in college football, also was on the line.

But trailing 28–7 early in the fourth quarter, it had become about pride for the Wolverines, led by fifth-year senior quarterback John Navarre. Navarre had been taking considerable heat because of his 0–6 record as the starting Michigan quarterback in road games against ranked teams. Talk before the game had been unpleasant, and many wondered if he lacked a fourth-quarter presence, particularly on the road and especially when the Wolverines trailed.

He offered proof of his abilities and later said the "monkey" was off the team's back, as he directed Michigan's largest comeback, leading the offense to 31 points in the fourth quarter for the miraculous 38–35 victory.

As if to say, "I told you so," quarterbacks coach Scot Loeffler said after the game, "He can come back."

And, boy, did he lead some kind of comeback. Navarre was 33-of-47 for 353 yards, two touchdowns, and one interception. Get this: he even scored on a 36-yard pass from receiver Steve Breaston for Michigan's first points in the opening drive of the second half.

In the end, the Wolverines may have been motivated by what tailback Chris Perry later called the "annoying" reminders of Navarre's road record against ranked teams. And in the end, Perry said, this was an enormous confidence-builder for Navarre and the Michigan offense.

How did they do it?

Michigan had played three poor quarters before finding its gear and rhythm in the fourth. They did it with a mixture of short passes from Navarre to tailback Chris Perry and a big play to receiver Braylon Edwards.

The Wolverines pulled to 35–28 when Edwards scored on a 52-yard pass from Navarre with 10:18 remaining. With just more than eight minutes left, Michigan got the ball back and Perry ended the drive with a 10-yard rushing touchdown to tie the game.

Minnesota went three-and-out on its next possession, and Michigan started is next series from its 42-yard line. Navarre converted on fourth down with a one-yard run. Perry fumbled on that drive, but the ball was recovered by tight end Tim Massaquoi, setting up Garrett Rivas' game-winning field goal. With 47 seconds left, Rivas made the 33-yard kick for the Wolverines' first lead of the game.

Perry entered that game as the nation's fifth-leading rusher, but the Wolverines had little success running the ball against the Gophers—Michigan had only 94 yards rushing. Perry caught 11 passes for 122 yards, including the 10-yard reception that started the rally.

In the fourth quarter, Navarre hit Edwards with a 52-yard pass and Perry with a 10-yarder.

"A lot changed that night in the second half," Perry later said. "It showed how much heart and pride we had within ourselves."

Michigan won five straight after that comeback, including wins against rivals Michigan State and Ohio State.

87 1995 Pigskin Classic: A 17-Point Late Comeback

Thirteen minutes left, 14th-ranked Michigan trailed 17–0 to Virginia in the 1995 season opener. This was the start of Lloyd Carr's first full season as head coach and redshirt freshman Scott Dreisbach's first game as the starting quarterback.

In those final 13 minutes of the Pigskin Classic at Michigan Stadium, Dreisbach dug deep and orchestrated three scoring drives for the 18–17 victory, at the time the biggest comeback in stadium history.

The clincher was Mercury Hayes' spectacular 15-yard touchdown reception in the right corner of the north end zone with no time remaining. The touchdown was the 16th play of Michigan's game-winning drive.

"I was basically concentrating on the ball and keeping my feet in bounds," Hayes would say of the touchdown reception. "I'm turning around looking at the ref. He pointed down and put up his arms. I was ecstatic...feeling good."

And then Hayes, who had seven catches for 179 yards, was swarmed by his teammates.

Who could tell during that comeback that Dreisbach was a redshirt freshman? Although he was booed early that game after the Wolverines failed to score the first three quarters, he remained poised and undeterred as he went 12-of-23 for 236 yards in the fourth quarter. For the game he was 27-of-52 for 372 yards, two touchdowns, and two interceptions.

While Hayes' touchdown catch was dramatic, the final seconds were equally so. With eight seconds left, Dreisbach threw short to receiver Tyrone Butterfield, who said he intentionally dropped the pass. Had he caught it short of the end zone, the game would have been over.

In that final huddle, Hayes made perfectly clear what should happen on the final play.

"That last play, we knew were going to win," Butterfield said. "Mercury looked at [Dreisbach] and said, 'I want the ball...I want the ball.'"

Amazingly, from Carr's vantage point on the sideline, he never saw the catch. He saw Dreisbach release the ball, and he saw the ball come down, but...

"It seemed like an eternity," Carr said. "The way the fans reacted, I knew we had scored."

The game must have felt like an eternity for Dreisbach. After throwing his second interception, there was no way he could have missed the boos from the packed stadium. There's also no way he could have missed backup Brian Griese warming up on the sideline. Dreisbach later said he never even considered he might be removed from the game. Carr said he planned to stick with his starter. "I never thought about taking him out all week," Carr said. "All week I told him, 'Don't look over your shoulder, there won't be anybody there.'"

Virginia, led by tailback Tiki Barber, who had an 81-yard touchdown run to give the Cavaliers a 14–0 lead, scored in each of the first three quarters.

Michigan's comeback started when Dreisbach and Hayes connected for a 41-yard pass to the Virginia 35. Ed Davis culminated the drive with a two-yard touchdown run to put Michigan on the board. Offensive lineman Joe Marinaro said after that score, the Wolverines were confident they would win.

"[Carr] said it would come down to the two-minute drill, and he was right," Marinaro said.

The Wolverines cut the deficit to 17–12 when Dreisbach threw six straight plays, including the 31-yard touchdown to Hayes. They missed the two-point conversion.

Surprisingly, Michigan failed to run the ball effectively in the opener and was held to 52 yards rushing. The Wolverines finished with 424 yards and the comeback victory.

88 The 1948 National Title

Sixty-some years later, it can be forgiven that Michigan fans might not remember the 1948 national championship.

Sure, everyone knows about the '47 team, the Mad Magicians, Fritz Crisler, the Rose Bowl, and the shellacking of USC that led to a post-bowl poll that elevated the Wolverines to the No. 1 ranking ahead of Notre Dame.

But 1948? Because of the Rose Bowl no-repeat rule, there would not be a second straight trip to the Rose Bowl for the Wolverines, although this version was just as worthy as the team the year before. Members of the 1948 Michigan team would later lament that without a postseason bowl appearance, the Wolverines' notoriety declined a bit since no one was writing about them.

This was Bennie Oosterbaan's first season as head coach, having made the transition as Fritz Crisler's handpicked successor. Crisler knew that Oosterbaan, the former three-time All-American at Michigan, would do all he could to maintain the single-wing offense.

Many thought Oosterbaan would be handicapped in terms of talent and experience in his first season. After all, only three offensive starters returned, and gone was Michigan's magnificent starting backfield of Howard Yerges, Jack Wiesenberger, Bob Chappuis, and Bump Elliott—the Mad Magicians.

Oosterbaan, then 42 years old, had only 34 players to work with, but there was a solid nucleus that included Gene Derricotte,

Bob Chappuis (49) of Michigan is hauled down by Dean Dill of USC after a seven-yard gain and a first down on USC's 15-yard line in the 1948 Rose Bowl. The Michigan player in the foreground is captain Bruce Hilkene.

Dick Rifenberg, Pete Elliott, and Alvin Wistert. Oosterbaan was an easygoing sort with a gentle soul, a complete departure from Crisler, whose style was much more dictatorial, commanding, and colder. Still, Oosterbaan's players later would talk endlessly about what a great motivator he had been.

He had enormous shoes to fill, but Oosterbaan didn't flinch during his first season. The Michigan program entered that season on a 14-game winning streak, dating back to the end of the 1946 season, and the Wolverines were defending national champions.

Oosterbaan made his head-coaching debut at Michigan State. The Wolverines needed a fourth-quarter touchdown—a five-yard run by fullback Tom Peterson—to win 13–7. They shut out Oregon and Purdue the next two games by a combined score of 54–0 and followed that with a rout of Northwestern, then ranked No. 3 nationally, 28–0. That win elevated the Wolverines three spots to the No. 1 ranking.

Two weeks later, however, the Wolverines dropped to No. 2 in the polls despite beating Illinois 28–20. The Illini had outgained Michigan in yardage, thus the demotion.

Michigan took out its frustrations the next two games, blanking Navy and then Indiana by a combined score of 89–0. The Wolverines were back on top of the national rankings and were riding a 22-game winning streak when they headed to Columbus to face Ohio State.

They completed a second straight perfect season with a 13–3 victory over the Buckeyes, their fourth straight. Michigan finished first in the conference and earned a second straight national championship.

Rifenberg, Elliott, and Wistert were named All-Americans, and Oosterbaan was voted National Coach of the Year, marking the first time two different coaches from the same school would earn the honor in back-to-back years.

89 The First Game Ever

Michigan football in its current state is played in an enormous stadium, features can't-miss winged helmets in maize and blue, and has an acclaimed marching band that performs one of college football's most recognizable fight songs, "The Victors."

Thanks to well more than 100 years of its football tradition, Michigan boasts the nation's winningest football record.

But when did Michigan start winning? Dig deep and the answer comes in May—yes, May, not what anyone would think of as perfect college football weather—of 1879.

Football? In May? In 1879?

Plenty was going on in the country then, so why not football? For instance, in 1879, the first five-and-dime store was opened by Frank Woolworth, milk was sold in glass bottles for the first time that

Brandy's Top Five

Jim Brandstatter, the former Michigan offensive lineman, is the analyst on radio broadcasts of Wolverines games. Here's a list of the five best Michigan games he's worked:

1. The 2004 triple-overtime game against Michigan State. Michigan won 45–37. "That's when I changed my mind about overtime. If you like great theater, every down, every snap of the ball, the anticipating grows higher and higher."

2. The 1998 Rose Bowl win against Washington State that clinched Michigan's perfect season and share of the national championship. "That game was one of the best."

3. Michigan's 27–21 win over Indiana on homecoming in 1979. Anthony Carter caught a 45-yard pass from John Wangler on the final play. "Oh, wow…Anthony's catch."

4. All of the Ohio State wins, especially 1996. "The one when Brian Griese hits Tai Streets and Shawn Springs slips. That was great."

5. Michigan's coach Lloyd Carr's first game in 1995, the comeback from 17 points down against Virginia. "Scott Dreisbach's touchdown pass to Mercury Hayes was absolutely memorable."

April, a meteor fell in Iowa, and Madison Square Garden opened in New York City. It also was a busy year for Thomas Edison, who on October 19 demonstrated electric light, then three days later perfected carbonized cotton filament light, and on December 31 gave his first public demonstration of an incandescent lamp.

Maybe Michigan's first-ever football game—against Racine College of Wisconsin at White Stockings Park in Chicago before 500 fans on May 30, a windy, extremely hot day, in what was more rugby than football as we now know it—didn't make the historical timeline of 1879, but it did make history for the Wolverines football program.

The Michigan-Racine game was described in a newspaper account in the *Chronicle*, Michigan's student newspaper, as "the finest game of Rugby foot-ball ever played this side of the Alleghenies."

Michigan's starting lineup that day included rushers Dave DeTar, Jack Green, Richard DePuy, and Irving Pond, halfback Charles Campbell, and goalkeeper Charles Mitchell.

Pond scored the team's first touchdown, and Michigan went on to win 1–0. DeTar, the team's first captain, added the point-after kick, but the referee said it missed. Even then, fans and players alike questioned the officiating, as the umpire, the Michigan team, and the spectators said the kick was good.

"However, we did not wish to dispute with the referee; yet, we must suggest he is as liable to be mistaken as anyone else," the *Chronicle* story said of the official's call.

Because this was not modern-day football, it is difficult to follow the newspaper account and even more difficult to find the highlights in a 1–0 win in the "two-inning" game, especially since DeTar actually successfully place-kicked again with two minutes remaining.

Most amusing about the game account is the fact that "friends of both teams were very enthusiastic and cheered lustily when an inch was made by either team." Hard to imagine a fan these days "cheering lustily" for the Wolverines over an inch gained, unless it was fourth-and-short.

According to the *Chronicle*, Michigan's team was treated in a "very courteous manner by Racine, and the best of feeling was displayed through the whole game." Michigan alumni in Chicago later honored the team at the Palmer House.

Michigan tied their other game, played in November.

90 Jim Brandstatter: Player, Analyst, Show Host

Since 1968, Jim Brandstatter has been deeply associated with Michigan football, first as a player, and these days as the game-day radio analyst and host of the coach's weekly television show.

Brandstatter, a former offensive lineman, was there at the beginning when the coach's show began in 1980 with Bo Schembechler, and in the mid-1980s he earned a radio presence working Michigan games. He partners with play-by-play announcer Frank Beckmann, who took over the radio duties after the death of the legendary Bob Ufer.

For Brandstatter, his job feels nothing like, well, a job.

"I try as best I can to not take it for granted," Brandstatter said. "I try as best I can to appreciate what I've had going. Probably what brings me back to that every day, every week, is when I see former players. When I see the Dan Dierdorfs, the Dick Caldarazzos, the Reggie McKenzies, the John Wanglers, the Tom Seabrons, who have done their thing, done their jobs away from Michigan, and they talk to me and tell me how lucky I've been to be part of the program.

"These are guys who've played in Super Bowls, are lawyers and doctors, and they all come back and talk about how lucky I am. I thank my lucky stars every day, mainly because I maintain those relationships with those guys and that's how I keep from not getting jaded and from not taking it for granted. I'm reminded every week from seeing someone what a lucky guy I've been to be part of this program for so long."

Brandstatter, however, takes exception to one thing.

"People have said to me, 'You are the voice of Michigan football,'" he said. "There has been one voice, and there never will be another one, and that was Bob Ufer. He was unique and a character, and by himself a huge force for Michigan football. Having grown up in that era, I believe there was no one better. There will never be another one."

The advent of radio technology has allowed Michigan fans to listen to Beckmann and Brandstatter's broadcasts even while on road trips sitting in opponents' stadiums watching the Wolverines. "Ear Radio," a radio worn on one ear, gives fans that opportunity. That way, they can hear what Brandstatter admits is a bit more of a biased take, while also getting injury and sideline updates related to the Wolverines.

"We're going to be fairly objective, but we're going to be biased toward Michigan because we're broadcasting to Michigan fans," Brandstatter said. "You have a certain bias toward that team—you broadcast to your clients. I think we do a good job being even-handed, but clearly you can tell in our voices that Frank and I are happier when Michigan is ahead.

"You lose credibility if you don't tell the truth, and people appreciate that. They can listen to you while you're rooting for Michigan, but they know you're going to be relatively objective."

91 Bob Chappuis: War Vet, UM Star

It isn't often that you leave your hometown of Toledo, enroll at Michigan, play a year of football, then get called up by the Army Air Force to serve your country at war, escape after being shot down, and then return to Michigan, eventually see your mug featured on the cover of *Time* magazine, and then help lead your team to a national championship.

Phew!

And those were just the early adulthood years of Bob Chappuis, a triple-threat back and a record-setter who was absolutely instrumental in helping the Wolverines to the 1947 national title.

He has one of those unique entries among Michigan's all-time players listed in the annual media guide. Chappuis earned a letter in 1942 and then in 1946 and 1947.

Chappuis, who was drawn to football after listening to his father's stories of his playing days at Denison in Ohio, started playing for Michigan as a sophomore in 1942. The *Time* cover story in 1947 later said that Bob Chappuis Sr. didn't care where his son chose to go to college "as long as it wasn't Ohio State. Dad just didn't like Ohio State."

But his college career was interrupted by service in the Army Air Force, and he was sent overseas to combat in World War II. He flew 21 missions as a radio operator and aerial gunner on B-25 bombers, and on February 13, 1945, his plane was shot down over Northern Italy. Chappuis and his fellow crewmen miraculously were able to parachute safely from the plane. They were 160 miles behind German lines, just north of the Po River, but were helped by Italian partisans who hid him and the two other crew members for the final three months of the war.

Chappuis, like many of his fellow enlisted men, returned to college and just happened to pick up where he had left off after his sophomore year. He led the conference in rushing and total offense in 1946 and was the team's Most Valuable Player. Fritz Crisler would later remark that Chappuis was very "coachable."

Things got even better in 1947 for the Wolverines, and Chappuis shined as a part of the famed Mad Magicians. He led the Wolverines that season and rewrote the Michigan record book, setting single-season records for touchdown percentage, yards per completion, and pass efficiency. He led Michigan and the conference in passing and total offense.

The week after Michigan defeated Illinois 14–7—the second of Michigan's two closest games that season, the other a 13–6 victory against Minnesota the week before—*Time* did a cover story on the Michigan football team. The magazine, dated November 3, 1947, featured an article about how to throw a football, and Chappuis' face was right there in the center of the cover.

Chappuis finished second in Heisman Trophy voting, and in the Wolverines' magical 49–0 Rose Bowl win over USC, he ran for 91 yards and threw for 188. The AP held another vote after that game, and Michigan was named national champion. Notre Dame had held the distinction after the post-regular-season vote.

"We won the Big Ten, and we got to go to the Rose Bowl, and I think we were content with that," Chappuis said later. "We didn't say, 'Well, we're better than Notre Dame.'"

Chappuis played two years of professional football after graduating from Michigan and then went into business. He died on June 17, 2012, at age 89.

92 The Upsetting App State Upset of 2007

Losses, of course, are never easy, but the season opener of 2007, a year full of promise with the return of top offensive players Chad Henne, Mike Hart, and Jake Long, was particularly heartbreaking for the Wolverines.

Then-fifth-ranked Michigan took a considerable amount of criticism from news outlets around the country after losing 34–32 to two-time defending I-AA champion Appalachian State at Michigan Stadium.

Hart, the team's top rusher, called it the "biggest loss" in Michigan history. Naturally, Mountaineers coach Jerry Moore had a different view and said it may be "one of the great victories in college football—maybe the greatest."

Appalachian State gained monumental coverage and reaped huge economic benefits from merchandise sales after the upset. Michigan also received monumental national coverage, but of a negative variety. Michigan rivals overwhelmed the Appalachian State bookstore with orders for Appalachian State T-shirts and apparel, and within hours of the upset, anti-Michigan fans had posted online their cell-phone videos from a variety of locations, like Beaver Stadium and Ohio Stadium, capturing the moment when Penn State and Ohio State fans heard that Michigan had lost.

The Mountaineers scored the go-ahead field goal, a 24-yarder by Julian Rauch following a 24-yard pass from Armanti Edwards to CoCo Hillary to the Michigan 5-yard line, with 26 seconds left. Michigan then had 21 seconds with which to work. On the second play from scrimmage, Henne connected on a 46-yard pass to Mario Manningham to set up a last-gasp field goal, a 37-yard attempt by Jason Gingell with six seconds left.

Gingell's kick was blocked by Corey Lynch after a protection breakdown, and Lynch, who recovered the ball, returned it 62 yards as the clock expired. The Wolverines watched in disbelief.

They had trailed 28–17 at halftime after the defense allowed 244 yards of total offense and an average of 7.6 yards per play. Appalachian State was efficient, converting on six of seven third downs. Meanwhile, the Wolverines looked out of sorts offensively. Henne was off his game, and Hart was sidelined in the second quarter with a thigh injury.

Michigan's defense improved in the second half. Shawn Crable forced a fumble by Edwards, setting up a scoring drive culminated by Hart's four-yard run. A two-point conversion failed, and the Wolverines trailed 31–26 at the end of the third quarter. With 4:36 left in the game, Hart scored again, this time on a 54-yard touchdown run. The two-point conversion failed, but Michigan led 32–31.

"I thought we had [the game]," Hart said. "We didn't do it. We didn't finish the game."

For a team that entered the season with high hopes, and for a team considered a legitimate player in the national-championship arena, losing to Appalachian State was a knock-out punch in Week 1 of the college football season.

Michigan coach Lloyd Carr, who endured heavy criticism after the loss, would not assign blame after the program's worst defeat.

"I thought we were not a well-prepared football team," Carr said. "That is my job, and I take full responsibility for that. We didn't execute. We simply made too many mistakes and had too many missed opportunities."

93 Be Part of the M Club

There are Michigan football fans galore within the state of Michigan and throughout the country. They go to games at Michigan Stadium, they follow the Wolverines on the road, or they listen to the games via radio or watch on television. They buy Michigan apparel and support the team in any way they can.

Fans who want to play a more active role, however, join a number of Michigan clubs. The University of Michigan Club of Detroit is the oldest, largest, and perhaps best known. It was founded in Detroit in 1895 and started with 170 members. Its goals were simple: to promote the university and host a banquet every year. The club still hosts the annual football "bust" at the conclusion of each regular season, and it also provides the coveted M Rings that are presented to the football seniors. The bust, which is open to the public, has had as many as 1,200 attendees.

Since not every Michigan football fan is an alumnus of Michigan, the club is open to anyone. "Anybody can join," said Lynn Evans, Michigan football's senior manager in 1957 and an M Club of Detroit member. Just look at Roger Simmons, a former club president who never attended Michigan. The only requirement is you must be a paid member of the Michigan Alumni Association, then visit the club's website—umclubgreaterdetroit.org—to join.

"Being a member is a must-do for a Michigan fan," Simmons said.

The club meets once a month, typically featuring a speaker from the University of Michigan. There is an annual golf outing at Radrick Farms, a Michigan golf course, and there are out-of-town football trips that were started at the request of former Michigan football coach and athletics director Fritz Crisler in the 1940s. The group also raises money to support the Club's scholarship fund at the university. And, of course, the Club hosts an annual football-season kickoff party.

The University of Michigan Club has come a long way since 1895. The group started the football bust in 1921 to honor coach Fielding Yost's team that finished 5–1–1. Perhaps that feeling of camaraderie at the bust had a residual effect—the next two teams won back-to-back Big Ten titles with a combined record of 14–0–1.

Crisler then worked with the Detroit Club to form the transportation committee. The goal was to gather fans to watch Michigan play football on the road and, ultimately, raise money for scholarship funds. That committee continues today, and is a major fund-raiser. Where does the money go? The Detroit Club currently grants 12 or more scholarships a year to athletic trainers, Michigan band members, and the general student population.

The Club has about 1,400 active members from the metro-Detroit area, but many of them who move from southeast Michigan maintain their membership.

"We have members from all over the country, and many come back for bust and the golf outing," Simmons said. "It's really a great thing to be a part of, and I think any Michigan fan would enjoy it."

94 The Incredible Michigan Band

Game days at Michigan Stadium are as much about the Michigan marching band as they are about the football team. After all, could you imagine a Saturday without hearing "The Victors" played with vigor and precision by the band?

Like the Wolverine football players, the Michigan marching band members spend countless hours in the off-season and during the school week practicing, perfecting the music that is so much a part of the Michigan tradition and game-day experience.

The finished product is what Michigan fans see on Saturdays—and, of course, in a smaller grouping at other athletic events when an edited version of the band performs. But football Saturdays are when the band is showcased in its top form.

Game day begins early for the band members. About four hours before kickoff, they begin practice at Revelli Hall and run through much of their pregame and halftime performances. The band then begins to make its way to the stadium about an hour or so before the game, as the members parade down Hoover Street, then left onto Greene Street, and then toward Michigan Stadium. It is an amazing sight as the band essentially becomes mingled with the fans on Hoover and Greene Streets as the mass of people make their way to the stadium.

The band heads toward the tunnel of Michigan Stadium where it stops, turns to the right, and plays "Let's Go Blue" and "The Victors." The group then enters the tunnel of Michigan Stadium, and when the band is ready to take the field, the drum major signals the stadium announcer, who then announces in a booming voice to the crowd, "Ladies and gentlemen, presenting the Michigan marching band! Band, take the field!"

The Michigan marching band is an essential part of the home-game experience in Ann Arbor. Photo courtesy of Per Kjeldsen.

The band marches onto the field to the "Entry Cadence" and then appears to spill out into lines that form the "Fanfare M." The band then plays the "M Fanfare," which consists of portions of "The Victors," "Varsity," and "The Yellow and Blue." At the end of the "M Fanfare," the drum major moves alone from the middle of the band to the 20-yard line in the north end of the stadium. The drum major then removes his hat, turns to face the other direction, and bends backward to touch his head to the ground, and it is "game on" from there.

Michigan's marching band grew from a grassroots student effort in the late 19th century when Harry dePont, an Ann Arborite, invited all musicians on campus to meet so that organization of the school's first band could begin. Nearly 30 musicians showed up for that meeting on November 13, 1896, and the first rehearsal was held. The student-run band, which received no financial support from the school, became a part of the football tradition in the fall of 1897.

For so many years, the Michigan marching band was an all-male organization, until 1972 when women were admitted. Naturally, the number of applicants increased, and now nearly half the membership is women.

95 Jon Jansen: Two-Time Captain

The Rock. That was his nickname. The Rock.

Professional wrestler? Financial advisor? Mountain climber?

No, Jon Jansen was "the Rock" because he was a tireless competitor at Michigan, a four-year presence at right tackle who started a program-record 50 games for the Wolverines and was one of the anchors of an offensive line that helped Michigan earn a share of the 1997 national championship.

He was a two-time captain, helping lead Michigan to back-to-back Big Ten titles in 1997 and 1998. Jansen earned Academic All–Big Ten honors twice and was the 1998 Big Ten Offensive Lineman of the Year. He was drafted in the second round of the 1999 NFL Draft by the Washington Redskins.

Jansen, who redshirted in 1994 as a tight end before being moved to right tackle, tied the offensive line starting mark held by Greg Skrepenak when he made his 48th career start against Ohio State on November 21, 1998. He nearly missed making his 49th start at Hawaii a week later because of an injury suffered to his left ankle in the game against the Buckeyes. Even with his Achilles tendon badly injured in the second quarter, Jansen continued to play against Ohio State in a 31–16 loss at Ohio Stadium.

"It was my last Big Ten game, my last game against Ohio State," he would later say. "No matter what happened, I was going to give it what I had."

He was the Rock, after all, and he was determined to make his 49th career start at Hawaii, tying Mark Messner's school record.

"There's a lot of things in life you can do by just showing up, but football's not one of them," Jansen said, explaining why he had no intention of starting the Hawaii game, then taking a seat to rest the ankle. "I've always believed that the team that gets more fired up has the best chance to win. You've got to have emotion. You've got to want to be out there."

Jansen, a 6'7", 300-pounder, earned the Michigan record for consecutive starts when he made his 50th against Arkansas on New Year's Day in the Florida Citrus Bowl. The Wolverines won 45–31, and Jansen went down in Michigan history.

It was a fitting finale for a player so respected by his teammates he was voted cocaptain in consecutive years.

The start of his senior season was a challenging one. The Wolverines were coming off the high of the special 1997 co–national championship season, but they opened the 1998 campaign with consecutive losses at Notre Dame and then at home against Syracuse. Jansen would be integral in challenging his teammates and drawing them together to march through the rest of the schedule.

"When you win all your games, it's not that hard to be a good leader," Jansen said, looking back at his captainship. "Everything falls into place. When things go bad, that's when you find out about yourself and your teammates."

The Wolverines rattled off eight straight wins. During the practice week before the Penn State game on November 7, Jansen and fellow cocaptain Juaquin Feazell, a defensive tackle, worked so hard against each other during practice that Jansen started a fight.

"You just watch [Jansen], and you know you've got to play better, play harder," said fullback Aaron Shea. "You don't want to let him down."

Jansen was considered the best NFL offensive line prospect to come out of Michigan since Jumbo Elliott, a second-round selection in 1988. What he lacked in overall size—yes, he was considered slightly light for a lineman—Jansen more than made up for in toughness, leadership, and work ethic.

Michigan coach Lloyd Carr didn't know when to stop heaping accolades on Jansen. He praised his "toughness, intelligence, integrity, consistency, and love for the game."

"I mean, he's special," Carr said.

No, he's the Rock.

96 UM-Texas Rose Bowl 2005

During the week leading up to the 2005 Rose Bowl, the Michigan defenders talked incessantly about their need to slow Texas quarterback Vince Young. It was not about stopping Young, because the Wolverines knew that would be impossible, but the key would be to slow the dual-threat quarterback, the type that had been giving Michigan fits all season.

Michigan fell in a 38–37 heartbreaker to Texas, an edge-of-your-seat-type game that featured five lead changes. The final lead came on a 37-yard-field goal made by Texas' Dusty Mangum as time expired to give the sixth-ranked Longhorns (11–1) the victory in their first-ever meeting with the Wolverines. Michigan's Ernest Shazor, got a hand on the ball, deflecting it ever-so-slightly.

Mangum would later say that he had imagined that very scenario during the two weeks of preparation for the bowl game.

"I thought I would go out there and kick the game winner, and that would be my only field goal of the game," he said.

While no one could have predicted such a finish to such a competitive game, everyone knew what Young was capable of doing. The Wolverines were unable to contain Young, who had 372 of Texas' 444 yards, and five touchdowns. Young had 21 carries for 192 yards and four rushing touchdowns, including a 60-yarder to open the second half.

"He killed us," Michigan senior cornerback Marlin Jackson said after the game. "It was Vince Young. We talked about it all week, about not letting him get out and keeping him bottled up inside—we just weren't getting him on the perimeter. We missed tackles, that's what killed us."

Michigan finished 9–3 overall and earned a share of the Big Ten title during the regular season, but the Wolverines' final two games of the season were devastating, particularly on defense. In the final regular-season game against rival Ohio State, dual-threat quarterback Troy Smith was dominant with 386 yards in a 37–21 win.

Offensively, the Wolverines were efficient. Chad Henne, who became the first freshman to start at quarterback in a Rose Bowl, was 18-of-34 for 227 yards, and his four touchdown passes tied a Rose Bowl record. Receiver Braylon Edwards, playing in his final game for Michigan, had 10 catches for 109 yards and was on the other end of three of those touchdown passes. Freshman tailback Mike Hart had 21 carries for 83 yards, and kicker Garrett Rivas had three field goals.

"If you score 37 points, it should be enough, but it wasn't," Michigan coach Lloyd Carr said. "We don't have any excuses."

Chad Henne prepares to throw in the Rose Bowl against Texas on January 1, 2005.

Perhaps the most impressive performance for the Wolverines was from receiver Steve Breaston, who gained 315 all-purpose yards, breaking O.J. Simpson's Rose Bowl record of 276 yards in 1969. Breaston had six kickoff returns for 221 yards, including a long of 53 yards, and he gave the Wolverines excellent field position all day. He also scored on a 50-yard reception.

After Texas took a 21–14 lead at the start of the second half on a designed run that Young took 60 yards for a touchdown, Michigan scored 17 unanswered points. The Wolverines took their first lead of the game, 28–21, with 6:29 left in the third quarter on Edwards' third touchdown, a nine-yard pass from Henne.

Michigan expanded its lead when linebacker Prescott Burgess intercepted Young, giving the Wolverines the ball at the Texas 45-yard line. But they could get no closer than the Texas 27 and settled for a 44-yard field goal by Rivas for their biggest lead of the game, 31–21.

That's when Young, 17–2 as a starter, kicked into gear. He scored two fourth-quarter touchdowns on runs of 10 and 23 yards, and he directed Texas' winning drive with just less than three minutes left.

"I guess I'm just a little tired of coming out here and losing," Breaston said. "I thought we played a good game, but they also played a good game. It's too bad someone had to lose—and we're on the losing end."

97. Rose Bowl 1989: Michigan-USC, Bo's Last Game

When Bo Schembechler walked off the field on November 25, 1989, his Wolverines having just beaten Ohio State 28–18, no one could have known that would be Schembechler's last game in Michigan Stadium.

Schembechler didn't really know either. Well, he *knew*, but he had not spent a lot of time dwelling on retirement, and he certainly didn't want some kind of circus-like sendoff, no farewell tour of the Big Ten or anything cheesy like that.

That was not Schembechler's style.

But when he walked through the tunnel to the locker room to celebrate with his team, which had become the first in 23 seasons to win back-to-back Big Ten football titles, Schembechler was fairly certain that at age 60, a survivor of two heart attacks—the first on the eve of his first Rose Bowl in 1970—and two quadruple-heart-bypass surgeries, he needed to slow down and put an end to 17-hour work days and those hyped-up Saturdays during football season.

He had been pushing it for years. He defied medical logic, but his physicians knew Schembechler could not maintain his pace and live a long life. Schembechler was a notoriously stubborn man, but even he knew the value of health.

"Something told me after the last Ohio State game I would not be back again," Schembechler said.

He had scheduled a team meeting on December 13. His plan was to first tell his team, and then have a news conference. But the news leaked. He told his players he would miss them more than anything. He also told them that, yes, the Rose Bowl against USC would be his last, but he didn't want them engaging in any kind of hokey, let's-win-one-for-Bo talk. This was their game, he told them. After all, they had done the work, gone 8–0 in the Big Ten, and earned the right to play on New Year's Day.

Not surprisingly, Schembechler's farewell was emotional.

"The hardest thing I've ever had to do is give up my football team, but I'm doing it because I think I've run my luck about as far as I can take it," Schembechler said, choking back tears. "This has been the greatest job I've ever had."

Schembechler was leaving coaching because he needed to give his heart and his body a rest. But he didn't plan to rest against USC. He was typical Schembechler—emotional, fiery—and he gave the officials an earful.

The Wolverines lost Schembechler's final game 17–10 to the Trojans. With the game tied 10–10 in the fourth quarter,

Schembechler got tricky. On fourth-and-2, he called for a fake punt, and freshman punter Chris Stapleton ran 24 yards for a first down at the USC 31. But a late flag had been thrown. The play was nullified, and Schembechler went ballistic. He said later that after looking at the play from all angles, it must have been a phantom hold, because he never saw it.

"They hurt a lot of kids with that call," Schembechler said of the officials. "Now, we didn't deserve to win that game, but without that call we could have won. We could have won, easily."

Schembechler insisted the official was "looking to make a bad call."

USC scored a touchdown with 1:10 left in the game. Schembechler's coaching career at Michigan ended with a 194–48–5 record. Through 21 seasons, he never had a losing record.

98 Rose Bowl 1993: Wheatley a Star

The Michigan Wolverines had a full year to think about the 1992 Rose Bowl.

They had been humbled by the faster Washington Huskies 34–14, and the loss hurt in a big way. So when the two were matched again in the 1993 Rose Bowl, the Wolverines had the perfect opportunity to make amends.

Washington had motivation, too. The Huskies would be seeking a third straight Rose Bowl victory, while Michigan hoped to preserve its unbeaten season. The Wolverines had gone 8–0–3 during the regular season, finishing with a disappointing 13–13 decision at Ohio State.

Michigan was a veteran group. The Wolverines' offensive line was led by seniors Steve Everitt, Joe Cocozzo, Doug Skene, and Rob Doherty; their quarterback was seasoned and experienced senior Elvis Grbac; and they also boasted a veteran tight end in Tony McGee. What they also had, though, was highly acclaimed tailback Tyrone Wheatley, only a sophomore from nearby Inkster, Michigan.

It was Wheatley who would provide an enormous spark for the Wolverines, leading them to a 38–31 victory over Washington. That win sealed a 9–0–3 record, their first undefeated season since 1973.

But without that offensive line, Michigan would never have gained 483 yards of offense, and Wheatley, voted the Rose Bowl's MVP, most certainly would not have rushed for 235 yards on 15 carries and scored rushing touchdowns of 56, 88, and 24 yards. In the days before the game, assistant coaches Les Miles and Mike DeBord worked with the linemen, dressed in street clothes, as they spent a number of extra hours running through plays in the parking lot across from the Huntington Beach hotel where the team stayed.

The coaches would later say that additional work undoubtedly helped.

To his credit, though, Wheatley was spectacular on the national stage, and his performance that day initiated talk of his potential Heisman Trophy candidacy the following year. His 88-yard touchdown run at the start of the third quarter set a Rose Bowl record.

Michigan started at its 12-yard line where Mercury Hayes was tackled on the kickoff return. The next play, with the hole opened wide by Joe Marinaro, Wheatley sprinted 88 yards for the score, giving Michigan a 24–21 lead.

"Joe just opened it up, and I went," Wheatley said.

Washington answered right back with a seven-play, 46-yard scoring drive that took only 2:32 and gave them the lead 28–24.

Entering the fourth quarter, it was 31–31, but the Wolverines' offense was in trouble. Wheatley was sidelined with lower-back

Tyrone Wheatley streaks in for another long touchdown run, this one for 56 yards in the second quarter, against Washington at the Rose Bowl on January 1, 1993.

spasms, and receiver Derrick Alexander was out with a pulled hamstring.

McGee caught the winning touchdown, a 15-yard pass from Grbac. McGee finished with 117 yards on six passes and also had a 49-yard touchdown reception. Grbac was 17-of-30 for 175 yards, two touchdowns, and no interceptions.

Before McGee's game-winning score, the Michigan defense had to come up with an enormous stop. Washington drove to the Michigan 5-yard line, but Shonte Peoples stuffed the Huskies the next three downs. Travis Hanson missed a 22-yard field goal attempt.

After the Wolverines took the lead, Washington moved the ball again, this time to the Michigan 25. Mark Brunell was sacked by Tony Henderson, and then Brunell threw two incompletions before being stopped two yards short on a fourth-down scramble.

"What meant the most was that nobody thought we could win the fourth quarter," said cocaptain and safety Corwin Brown. "Now people can judge us as a great team. We never lost a game."

It was Michigan's first Rose Bowl win since 1989.

"I kept asking the team, 'What did we come here for?'" Michigan coach Gary Moeller said. "What did we come here for? To sing 'The Victors' in Pasadena, and we did it."

99 Forest Evashevski: Crisler's Greatest QB

By the time Forest Evashevski was a senior in high school at Detroit's Northwestern High, it was pretty clear he had every right to pursue the game at the next level.

But in the second game of his senior season, he suffered a cerebral hemorrhage. "They did three spinal taps on me before they decided to operate. I was supposed to be through with football," he told the *Detroit News*. "But when something is taken away from you like that, I believe you want it even more than you did before."

His desire to play college football never waned.

Evashevski's father could not afford to send him to college, so the young high school graduate began working for the Ford Motor Company, and he earned a spot on their industrial football team. He saved his money and enrolled at Michigan 18 months later. While there, he spent his summers as a dock hand and washed dishes and parked cars to help pay his way.

Fritz Crisler was in his first season as Michigan's head coach when Evashevski arrived to play football for the Wolverines in 1938. Because the Wolverines already had a center, Evashevski was moved to quarterback a week before his first game. Playing quarterback in the single-wing mostly meant calling signals and blocking for the running back.

Evashevski, who always seemed to understand what Crisler wanted from his offense, started three straight seasons and helped Tom Harmon earn the Heisman Trophy in 1940.

"As a blocker," Harmon once said of Evashevski, "I never saw a better one."

Evashevski was a true leader, emotional but also lighthearted with a mischievous streak. He captained the 1940 team and he was able to have some fun with Crisler, a strict disciplinarian who never became that close to his players during their playing careers.

During one game that Michigan led 21–0 at halftime, Crisler worried the Wolverines might let down, so he ordered the team—as he often did—to consider the game scoreless. Having issued that order, Crisler then asked Evashevski the score.

"You can't kid me, Coach. The score is 21–0," he replied.

Evashevski called Crisler "Chris Fisler" and couldn't resist the urge to tease the coach.

During a pregame speech against Minnesota, Crisler told the players he wanted "11 tigers on defense and 11 lions on offense." Evashevski raised his hand and said he would not play unless he could be a leopard.

Crisler was one for punctuality. He demanded it of himself and his players. He showed up for practice a few minutes late one day, and Evashevski let him have it. "Fritz," he said, "we begin practice at 3:30. It's now 3:35. Take a lap around the field." Crisler took the lap.

It was Harmon's 21st birthday on September 28, 1940, when the Wolverines readied to play at California. As the players huddled before the opening kickoff, Evashevski waved Harmon out of the huddle and asked the team to give him a birthday present.

"Everybody knock somebody down," he said.

And they did. Harmon went 94 yards on the opening kickoff for a touchdown against California. Happy birthday!

The Wolverines were 19–4–1 during Evashevski's three years, and Crisler later called him the "greatest quarterback I ever had."

Evashevski won the Big Ten Medal, given to the school's top senior student-athlete. He was the senior class president at Michigan and an honor society member. He eventually went into coaching and became Iowa's 19th head coach. Evashevski died on October 30, 2009, at age 91.

100 Win over Notre Dame in 1986

Six years later, and it felt like Bo Schembechler and the Michigan Wolverines got what they believed they were due at Notre Dame Stadium.

In 1980 Michigan appeared to be on its way to a victory at Notre Dame when suddenly everything changed. Harry Oliver made a 51-yard field goal, the kick low, hard, and into a 15 mph wind to lift Notre Dame over Michigan, 29–27. Irish luck?

So in 1986, when Notre Dame kicker John Carney came out to attempt a 45-yard field goal with 17 seconds left that would win the game, Schembechler believed that this time, the luck would be with the Wolverines and not the Irish.

Carney's attempt was long enough but hooked left. Michigan would hold on for the 24–23 win in a wild one at Notre Dame Stadium.

"I knew Carney would miss," Schembechler said after the game. "This was my turn."

For first-year Notre Dame coach Lou Holtz, this would be a crushing loss in his debut.

Going into the game, Schembechler believed the Wolverines were familiar enough with Holtz's style, since they had seen it while he coached at Minnesota. But Holtz had different personnel available to him at Notre Dame, and that invited a different way to scheme.

Holtz's game plan for Michigan would be wide open, as if to open wide all the eyes watching the game, considering the Irish were unranked against the third-ranked Wolverines.

The Irish did gain 455 yards, averaged 6.3 yards a play, had 27 first downs, and were 8-of-12 on third-down conversions. To be sure, Schembechler did not like his defense questioned after the game.

"Lou Holtz is a very diverse offensive coach, and he kept us off balance with so many different formations," he said. "We were in hostile territory. We came out with a victory. I don't care how you come with them."

Notre Dame might have played a wide-open offense, but the game was marred by turnovers. The Irish turned the ball over four times, including three inside the Michigan 15-yard line. Turnover one: two minutes into the second half, flanker Reggie Ward fumbled at the Michigan 7-yard line, and safety Tony Gant recovered. Turnover two: with 8:57 left in the third quarter, Notre Dame muffed a return of a Michigan kickoff, and UM safety Doug Mallory recovered it at the Irish 27. Turnover three: fullback Pernell Taylor fumbled at Michigan's 15, and Mallory made the recovery with a minute left in the third quarter. Turnover four: with 10:54 to play, Michigan cornerback David Arnold intercepted Steve Beuerlein's eight-yard pass into the end zone.

"We did self-destruct," Holtz would later say.

Michigan had its moments, too, to open the door for Notre Dame's last-gasp attempt to win. With 1:33 remaining, Michigan's Bob Perryman fumbled at the Notre Dame 26-yard line, and linebacker Wes Pritchett recovered. Beuerlein then completed passes of 33 and 16 yards to move Notre Dame to the Michigan 28. And then…the kick.

"I turned to Mike Reinhold on the sideline and said, 'Mike, he's going to make it,'" Michigan quarterback Jim Harbaugh said after the game. "He said, 'Hey, suck in that stomach, Jimmy. No way. No way.'"

Notre Dame went into halftime with a 14–10 lead.

Coming out of the half, Michigan took the kickoff and drove 78 yards. Tailback Jamie Morris scored on a one-yard run. Then Mallory recovered the muffed kickoff, and Harbaugh found Morris for a 27-yard touchdown in a six-second drive to build a 24–10 lead.

"I've never caught a ball that far downfield," Morris said of his touchdown reception. "It was a throw-back play where the back just runs downfield down the sideline. That was a big thrill."

Harbaugh was 15-of-23 for 239 yards and a touchdown. Morris rushed for 77 yards and caught three passes for 31 yards. He would become the first tailback since 1900 to score three touchdowns against the Irish, two on runs.